Beautiful Boards
& Delicious
Charcuterie
for Every Occasion

Beautiful Boards
& Delicious
Charcuterie

for Every Occasion

FOX CHAPEL
PUBLISHING

KATE WOODSON

© 2023 by Kate Woodson and Fox Chapel Publishing Company, Inc., 903 Square Street, Mount Joy, PA 17552.

Recipe selection, design, and book design © Fox Chapel Publishing. Recipes and photographs © G&R Publishing DBA CQ Products.
Additional studio photography by Mike Mihalo: 51, 77, 107, 115
Additional recipes by Aubrey Vonada: 50, 76, 106, 114

ISBN 978-1-4971-0383-2

Library of Congress Cataloging-in-Publication Data is on file with the Library of Congress.

To learn more about the other great books from Fox Chapel Publishing, or to find a retailer near you, call toll-free 800-457-9112 or visit us at *www.FoxChapelPublishing.com*.

We are always looking for talented authors. To submit an idea, please send a brief inquiry to acquisitions@foxchapelpublishing.com.

Printed in China
First printing

25

51

Index

Introduction

What is a charcuterie board? If you're picking up this book, chances are you've heard the term and you're a bit curious. Or, you're already well-versed in the topic and want some fresh ideas. You might have even picked it up because charcuterie boards—and the other recipes mentioned in this book—are beautiful, inviting, and intriguing. You may want to ask someone: are food boards really just that? A board with food on it? I'm here to show you that the answer is yes, but it takes a lot more than ingredients and a spare board to make a truly successful spread. In this book, you will learn—or reaffirm—the skills needed to craft a beautiful board for every gathering.

The word "charcuterie" is a French term that refers to cold cooked, cured, or smoked meats. While there are plenty of meat-based boards in this book (the Meat Lovers board on page 28, for instance), charcuterie boards don't stop there. The popularized and well-loved version of a charcuterie board includes a variety of cheeses, nuts, vegetables, breads, and crackers. The off-board components include dips, spreads, jams, salsas, and more. And we have also included recipes for butter boards, which taste just as delicious as the name suggests.

Many people—including the talented and creative contributors to our gallery—like to theme their boards to the occasion. Valentine's Day, Thanksgiving, Birthdays, Christmas...name an occasion, we have a beautiful board to show you!

I hope you find joy and comfort in the boards, accompaniments, dips, and spreads that are in this book. And if you take just one thing away from the recipes, let it be this: have fun with it!

—*Kate*

Gallery of Beautiful Boards

In this gallery of beautiful boards, you will find handcrafted boards made by a variety of talented, passionate, and creative contributors. This selection shows that you really can make a board for every occasion!

Title: The Ultimate Entertainer Board

Creator: Olive and Honey (@olive.and.honeyy)

This board is sure to be a crowd pleaser! With a mix of gouda, Manchego, asiago, and Brie, there's something for everyone! Berries and a few sweet treats give this board the true meaning of savory and sweet!

Title: Happy Birthday Board

Creator: Alisha Wolfson (@biglittleboards)

What better way to celebrate your birthday than with cheese and charcuterie! We made sure to include different meats and cheeses with a variety of flavors, textures, ages, and colors. And of course, we included our favorite accompaniments.

Title: It's My Birthday Board

Creator: Lowcountry Board Babes (@lowcountryboardbabeshhi, lowcountryboardbabes.com)

This board is perfect for any kid's birthday party. Not all kids like birthday cake, so why not give them a customized char-"cute"-rie board? From cupcakes, cookies, and fruit to gumballs and gummy bears, this board is sure to please kids of all ages. It has what all kids want, sugar, but also the fruits they love: apples, grapes, and Cuties. We like to keep it festive but yummy at the same time!

Title: The Gathering Board

Creator: The Board Couple LLC (@theboardcouple)

A curated board with a nut mix base, charcuterie, artisan cheeses, fresh fruit, dried fruit, chocolates, antipasto, European-style mustard, preserve, honeycomb, and crackers all carefully arranged on our signature wooden boards. Each board is cut and handcrafted by our carpentry team.

Title: Let's Share! (Thanksgiving Edition)

Creator: Treats by Aly LLC (@treatsbyalynj, Treatsnj.com)

The perfect addition to your holiday gatherings and family reunions. Featuring a selection of premium cheeses such as Humboldt Fog, Truffle double Brie, and creamy Toscano cheese dusted with cinnamon, plus charcuterie and much more.

Title: Thanksgiving Dinner App Board

Creator: Lowcountry Board Babes (@lowcountryboardbabeshhi, lowcountryboardbabes.com)

This board is a perfect appetizer to have while preparing your Thanksgiving meal. It has a turkey-shaped Brie with cinnamon-pear jam, homemade white chocolate macadamia nut cookies, and spicy pimento cheese in the corner. It is a perfect balance of sweet and savory to stretch the bellies before the big meal.

Title: 'Tis the Season Board

Creator: Lowcountry Board Babes (@lowcountryboardbabeshhi, lowcountryboardbabes.com)

This board is perfect for all your holiday festivities. Keeping with the theme of the holidays, we've incorporated the Christmas tree Brie with apple-cinnamon jam, red and green caprese, homemade sausage balls, and homemade sugar spiced pecans.

Title: The Perfect Holiday Gathering Board

Creator: Boards by Courtney (@boardsbycourtney)

This board is perfect for your holiday gatherings, and sure to be a crowd-pleaser! Full of a wide variety of cheeses and charcuterie for all palates, this board features festive details to complete the look.

Title: Hot Cocoa Board

Creator: Lowcountry Board Babes (@lowcountryboardbabeshhi, lowcountryboardbabes.com)

Everybody loves a good hot chocolate during the holidays! This board comes with all the fixings and our recipe for Crock-Pot™ hot chocolate. Perfect for kids' parties or neighborhood gatherings. (Can also be spiked with your favorite holiday spirit.)

Title: Sorta Healthy Halloween Board

Creator: Lowcountry Board Babes (@lowcountryboardbabeshhi, lowcountryboardbabes.com)

Everybody needs a snack before trick-or-treating. This board features homemade sausage balls, pumpkin-shaped Brie with cinnamon-pear jam, pimento cheese, and lemon zest hummus. This board was created with sweets but also some crunchy low-carb options.

Title: Char-BOO-terie Board

Creator: Loryn Purvis, owner of Picnic Grazing Co. (@picnicgrazingco)

This Char-BOO-terie Board by Picnic Grazing Co. is the perfect centerpiece for your Halloween table.

Title: Brie Mine

Creator: Charcuterie Chick® (@charcuterie_chick)

The perfect Valentine's Day inspiration—a vibrant and festive heart-shaped arrangement with cheese hearts, salami roses, festive reds, and chocolate galore. This board is sure to impress your significant other! (Features Blake Hill Preserves, Columbus Craft Meats, and Supreme Brie.)

Title: Galentine's Day Board

Creator: Treats by Aly LLC (@treatsbyalynj, Treatsnj.com)

Double Brie, Manchego, creamy Toscano, prosciutto, Italian dry salami, sweet soppressata, and a mixture of fruit and nuts are some of the ingredients that make this platter the perfect Galentine's Day charcuterie board.

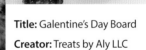

Title: An Afternoon Delight Board

Creator: Terrie's Luxe Charcuterie Boards (@Terriesluxecharcuterie)

Brimming with color and flavor, this Afternoon Delight board is perfect for spending time with friends and family!

Board Basics

Whether you're planning to make a board for a family gathering, a party, a picnic, or more, it will be the center of attention. Not only does a board feed everyone, but it also acts as a centerpiece and talking point for your event. With bright colors, different themes, and delicious accompaniments, boards are a must-have for entertainers. And the beauty of making a board is that it doesn't have to be difficult or time-consuming to put together; all it takes are some great ingredients and a little imagination.

Each board and recipe in this book are meant to inspire, so don't be afraid to create your own variations based on your preferences and what's available to you. After all, it's your board, so build it how you like it. Within these pages you will find recipes for classic charcuterie boards, sweet dessert boards, butter boards, dips, crackers, and so much more. It can be easy to get overwhelmed by all the "rules" out there on how to build the perfect board, but it all boils down to three factors. Take these into consideration, and your board will be destined for deliciousness!

Flavor

Cater to palates of all kinds by including a variety of flavors ranging from sweet to salty. Try to find a good balance between light and rich flavors. This allows everyone to build their own pairings and bites.

Texture

The texture of food has a lot to do with both the flavor and overall eating experience. The best boards use contrasting textures to play off each other. Crispy and creamy, crunchy and smooth, and so on.

Aesthetics

A nice presentation leads to an enjoyable eating experience. This doesn't mean every board has to be a work of art, but a thoughtful arrangement and a pop of color go a long way when it comes to creating a good-looking board.

Elements of a Board

Before you assemble your board, it's important to consider the key elements that make a board appealing to everyone at the table. The goal is to not only make a board that looks delicious, but that has balanced textures, flavors, and off-board extras as well. It feels like the possibilities are endless with such bountiful boards, but here is a list of the most common elements that help make a board beautiful.

Charcuterie

Here you'll want to follow the same logic as the cheese. Variety in terms of texture, style, and type of meat will lead to a delicious board. Include an assortment of mild, medium, and bold flavors. As always, include what you like and what's available in your area.

Cheeses

Variety is the key to a delicious cheese board. Include variety in the type of milk, strength of flavor, softness or firmness of texture, and style of cheese. Branch out and try cheeses you've never tried before. The most important thing is to include cheeses you like to eat.

Bread & Crackers

These are the vehicle on which to build the perfect bite. Crackers are a common choice, but fresh bread, toasted bread, and pretzels also make great options.

Butters and Spreads

A board dedicated to a base like butter, or a different kind of spread, can either be the star of the show or act as a stunning sidekick. Butter boards are filled with softened butter, like the name suggests, topped with delicious ingredients like spices, herbs, vegetables, and more. Accompany your spread-centered board with crunchy or soft scooping tools, like crackers, chips, or bread. And remember, you can make the board as decorative as you like!

Condiments & Dips

Jams, preserves, and chutneys bring a pop of color and sweetness to a board. Mustards add acidity and spice. While these are classic standbys, you don't have to stop there. Get creative with flavors by adding salsa, hummus, veggie dip, or anything else that comes to mind!

Garnishes

A little garnish will go a long way in adding flair and flavor to your board. Fresh herbs like rosemary, mint, sage, basil, parsley, or thyme make great additions.

Accompaniments

This is where the board gets its personality. Fruits like grapes or apples are commonly used to add a touch of sweetness and brighten up the board. Nuts bring some protein and crunch. Pickled items like sweet gherkins, baby dills, or olives have acidic and briny flavors that balance out the rich flavors of the meats and cheeses.

Serving Tips

The board is sure to taste delicious, but there are a few other aspects to be prepared for so the experience is a true success for your guests.

Portions

A good guideline is to assume that each guest will eat about 2 ounces of meat. However, if the board is the main food being offered, you may want to double that amount. The same rule applies to the amount of cheese to provide. Be sure to provide plenty of bread, crackers, and accompaniments to make sure everyone gets their fill.

Setting Your Table

While boards are beautiful, they also need to be easy to eat. Make sure to provide all the essential serving utensils so guests can easily enjoy the board. Spoons for jams, knives for cheese, forks for olives, and so on.

Use Labels

Labels are a great way to let people know what they're slicing into, especially if you've provided a few items that are a little out of the ordinary. Also, be sure to keep in mind any food allergies or sensitivities that your guests might have and label accordingly.

Board Presentation

The food itself will be beautiful to look at, but try adding a little something special to make it pop, such as grape bunches, chocolate-covered strawberries, and fun folded meats!

Making a flower out of meat, radishes, or even adding a real flower to your board will catch everyone's eye. For a meat flower like the one shown above, fold circular meat around the inside rim of a wine glass, place upside down on the plate, and pull the glass away to reveal your flower!

Delicious Meat and Cheese Pairings

Meat and cheese are the bases of most boards, but adding foods nearby that pair well with these classic cuts will bring harmony and balance to both the board and your taste buds. And don't forget to add crunchy bread or crackers to help create the perfect bite!

Fruits

Fresh fruit adds sweetness that pairs well with salty cheeses and meats. Try some of these combinations to freshen up your board!

Pears and brie	Melon and prosciutto
Blueberries and feta	Apples and salami
Grapes and gouda	Strawberries and spicy pepperoni

Nuts

Nuts add crunchiness to your board that soft meats and cheeses need. They're also easy to sprinkle around the board!

Pecans and brie	Cashews and roast beef
Pistachios and parmesan	Almonds and pork
Cashews and blue cheese	Walnuts and bacon

Briny Snacks

You might also like to have a pickled or briny snack on your board that will combat bold flavors with a delicious tang. Try some of these combinations!

Kalamata olives and feta	Sweet gherkins and summer sausage
Dill pickles and sharp cheddar	Pepperoncini and salami
Pickled cherries and blue cheese	Cured chorizo and pickled jalapeños

Crackers and Breads

Now that you have the ingredients, pile them on top of a crunchy piece of bread or cracker to complete the perfect bite!

Butter crackers and pepper jack	Toasted baguette and genoa salami
Cinnamon raisin bread and white cheddar	Woven wheat crackers and mortadella
Tortilla chips and Manchego	French bread and deli roast beef

Wine

What could be a more classic pairing than cheese and wine? To add an extra layer to your board experience, take care to pair your cheese with the best wine for the occasion. Look at our chart for some delectable ideas!

Note: Feel free to substitute sparkling cider or non-alcoholic wine for anyone who doesn't drink.

White Wine
Brie
Gouda
Swiss

Red Wine
Brie
Cheddar
Parmesan

Sparkling Wine
Gruyere
Feta
Monterey Jack

How to Build Your Board

While assembling a board isn't an exact science, it is helpful to have a process. It's best to start by placing the larger items and finish by nestling in the smaller items. This makes it easy to fill in any gaps left on the board.

Build a Foundation

Start by placing any bowls you'll need on the board. Fill small bowls with pickled items, mustards, jams, or dips and arrange them on the board. This saves you from trying to squeeze them on the board later. It also helps provide a foundation from which to build the rest of your board.

Cheeses & Meats

Space the cheeses evenly around the board. While it's not necessary to slice all the cheese, it can be helpful to cut a few slices to give guests a starting point. Now add any meat to the board. Get creative with different ways of folding, piling, and slicing meats.

Crackers & Bread

3 Add a few stacks and piles of crackers throughout the board. Don't worry about lining them up perfectly; randomness just adds to the rustic charm of the board. If you have larger slices of bread, add a small breadbasket or cutting board adjacent to the main board.

Add the Accompaniments

4 Plate any dips or butter boards you have created and nestle in the extras. Fill in any remaining gaps with nuts, dried fruit, veggies, pickles, fresh fruit, herbs, and whatever else you'd like. It's alright if things on the board touch – you're going for a full, abundant look here. Plus, the foods are meant to be paired together anyway, so you'll just be one step ahead.

Have fun with it! Don't fret over placing everything perfectly on the board. It all tends to fall into place just as the first guests arrive.

Dip Tips

Another great addition to a charcuterie or cheese board is a dip. Throughout this book, you will find complimentary dips to go with each board—but feel free to mix and match as you see fit!

Make Them Ahead

Most cold dips can be made hours ahead of time, then just pull them out of the fridge and serve. Plus, most cold dips taste better when they've had some time to chill, so it's basically a win-win. Hot dips can also be made ahead of time, just premix the ingredients and toss in the fridge until you're ready to heat them up.

Keep Them Hot

Slow cookers are an obvious choice for keeping dips hot, but not all dips are meant to be served in a slow cooker. If you're serving a baked dip, wrap towels or hot pads around the skillet or baking dish for extra insulation.

Keep Them Cold

It's important to keep cold dips cold—especially if you're serving mayo- or dairy-based dips on a hot day! To keep your dip chilled, just fill a larger bowl with ice and nestle your serving dish on top.

Keep Them Fresh

Add crunchy toppings and fresh garnishes to dips right before serving. If you're traveling, just bring your toppings along and finish the dip when you arrive. If you need to make an avocado-based dip ahead of time, press plastic wrap against the surface of the dip to eliminate air exposure. This should minimize any browning.

Savory

The board ideas in this section
will focus on more savory flavors;
you'll find smoky and salty
meats and cheeses, and dips and
accompaniments to compliment
or offset those tastes. These boards
also each have a theme that you
can tailor to whatever occasion
you are using a beautiful board
for. Remember to have fun when
arranging the food on your board.
Make it look interesting and artful.

Southern Belle Board

The sweet and sassy Southern Belle Board is the perfect mix of hot spices and sweet fruits. The Pimento Cheese dip ties it all together!

Cheeses: Pimento Cheese (*recipe below*), sharp cheddar, Muenster
Charcuterie: Black Forest ham, browned andouille sausage
Bread & Crackers: crackers, pretzel chips
Accompaniments: dill pickle spears, pecans, roasted peanuts, peaches, strawberries, grape tomatoes
Condiments & Dips: orange marmalade
Garnish: parsley

1. Put the Pimento Cheese, pickles, and orange marmalade in bowls and place them on and around the board.
2. Arrange the sharp cheddar, Muenster, Black Forest ham, and andouille sausage on the board.
3. Nestle in a few stacks of crackers and pretzel chips.
4. Fill in any remaining gaps with pecans, roasted peanuts, peaches, strawberries, and grape tomatoes.
5. Garnish with fresh parsley and serve.

Pimento Cheese

- 2 cups grated sharp cheddar cheese
- 1 (*8 ounce*) package cream cheese, softened
- ½ cup mayonnaise
- 4 ounces chopped pimentos (*drained*)
- ½ teaspoon garlic powder
- ½ teaspoon dried onion flakes
- ¼ teaspoon paprika
- ¼ teaspoon salt
- ¼ teaspoon black pepper

Combine ingredients with an electric mixer. Place in an airtight container and refrigerate for at least 2 hours to allow the flavors to develop.
Serves 8

Pimento Cheese

Orange & Avocado Salsa

- 1 orange, peeled & diced
- 1 jalapeño, seeded & finely chopped
- 1 cup chopped fresh cilantro
- 2 tablespoons orange juice
- ½ teaspoon salt
- 2 avocados, peeled & diced

In a mixing bowl, combine the orange, jalapeño, cilantro, orange juice, and salt. Add the avocado and gently stir to combine. Serve immediately with tortilla chips.
Makes about 3 cups

Corn & Bacon Dip

- 6 strips bacon, chopped
- 3 cups frozen corn, thawed
- ½ cup diced onion
- ¼ cup diced red bell pepper
- 1 jalapeño, seeded & diced
- 1 (*4 ounce*) package cream cheese, cubed and softened
- ¼ cup sour cream
- 2 green onions, thinly sliced
- 1 teaspoon sugar
- ¼ teaspoon salt
- ½ teaspoon black pepper

Cook bacon until brown and crispy, about 6 to 8 minutes. Transfer to a paper-towel-lined plate to cool and drain the excess grease.
In a large mixing bowl, combine bacon, corn, onion, bell pepper, jalapeño, cream cheese, sour cream, green onions, sugar, salt, and black pepper. Refrigerate for at least 1 hour before serving to allow the flavors to develop. Serve with crackers or tortilla chips.

Serves 8

Meat Lovers Board

This board is every meat lover's dream. Smoky, salty, and savory meats combine with crispy bites and spicy spreads. The result? A charcuterie board for the ages.

Cheeses: Gouda
Charcuterie: Pepperoni, mortadella, Genoa salami, soppressata salami, peppered salami, beef sticks, prosciutto
Bread & Crackers: crackers, Parmesan-Cheddar Crisps (*recipe below*)
Condiments & Dips: Refrigerator Pepper Jam (*recipe page 30*), stone-ground mustard
Garnish: parsley

1. Put the Refrigerator Pepper Jam and stone-ground mustard in small bowls and place them on the board.
2. Arrange the Gouda, pepperoni, mortadella, Genoa salami, soppressata salami, peppered salami, beef sticks, and prosciutto on the board.
3. Nestle in a stack of crackers and some Parmesan-Cheddar Crisps.
4. Garnish with parsley and serve.

Parmesan-Cheddar Crisps

- ½ cup grated parmesan
- ½ cup grated cheddar

Heat the oven to 350° and line a baking sheet with parchment paper. In a mixing bowl, combine the cheeses. Spread about 1 tablespoon of the cheese in a thin circle on the parchment paper; repeat with the remaining cheese. Bake 12 to 15 minutes or until the cheese is golden brown. Cool on the baking sheet before serving. Store in an airtight container for up to 1 week.

Makes about 18 crisps

Tip:
For added flavor, toss the cheese with your choice of seasonings before baking. Garlic salt, paprika, and ranch seasoning are all great options.

Refrigerator Pepper Jam, page 30

Parmesan-Cheddar Crisps

Refrigerator Pepper Jam

- 1 finely chopped red bell pepper
- 1 finely chopped yellow bell pepper
- 1 finely chopped orange bell pepper
- 2 finely chopped and seeded jalapeños
- 1 (*1.75 ounce*) package fruit pectin
- ¾ cup distilled white vinegar
- 4 cups sugar

Combine ingredients in a saucepan over medium heat. Bring the mixture to a boil for 5 minutes, stirring frequently. Add 4 cups of sugar and bring the mixture back to a boil; let boil for 2 minutes. Remove the pan from the heat and pour the jelly into containers. Allow to cool uncovered for 30 minutes. Seal and place in the refrigerator to allow the jelly to set. Refrigerate in an airtight container for up to 1 month. Serve with crackers, or pair with cream cheese for a classic appetizer.
Makes 5 cups

Flamin' Sausage Queso

- ½ pound spicy pork sausage
- ¾ cup chicken broth
- 16 ounces Velveeta (*cubed*)
- ½ cup shredded Pepper Jack cheese
- 1 (*14.5 ounce*) can Mexican-seasoned tomatoes (*undrained*)
- 1 cup black beans (*drained & rinsed*)
- ¼ cup chopped fresh cilantro

Preheat oven to 350°. Brown spicy pork sausage, crumbling it while it cooks; drain and dump into a 2-quart baking dish. Stir in chicken broth, Velveeta, Pepper Jack, tomatoes, and black beans. Bake for 30 minutes, or until the cheese is melted and everything is nice and hot. Stir in cilantro. Serve with nacho-cheese-flavored tortilla chips.

Slow cooker instructions: To make in a slow cooker, simply toss the browned and drained pork with the other ingredients into a 2-quart cooker; heat on high for 2 to 3 hours.

Serves a crowd

Hint of Smoke Board

The Hint of Smoke Board gives you everything you need: a mix of crunchy and soft textures, bite-sized snacks, and delicious, smoky flavors that will leave you wanting just one more bite!

Cheeses: smoked black pepper Gouda, smoked cheddar
Charcuterie: smoked beef sticks, grilled smoked kielbasa, mesquite-smoked turkey
Bread & Crackers: toasted baguette slices, butter crackers
Accompaniments: dill pickles, Bacon-Wrapped Stuffed Apricots (*recipe below*), almonds, pistachios, raspberries
Condiments & Dips: cherry preserves
Garnish: sage

1 Put the beef sticks, pickles, and cherry preserves in bowls and place them on the board.
2 Arrange the smoked Gouda, smoked cheddar, smoked kielbasa, and smoked turkey on the board.
3 Nestle some toasted baguette slices and butter crackers on the board.
4 Fill in any remaining gaps with Bacon-Wrapped Stuffed Apricots, almonds, pistachios, and raspberries.
5 Garnish with fresh sage and serve.

Bacon-Wrapped Stuffed Apricots

- 18 bacon strips
- ½ cup chopped walnuts
- ¾ cup crumbled blue cheese
- ½ teaspoon dried sage
- 36 dried apricots

Preheat oven to 400°. In a skillet, partially cook the bacon over medium heat for 6 minutes or until just brown but not crisp. Drain on paper towels and cut each strip in half.

Reserve 2 tablespoons of drippings in the skillet. Cook walnuts in the drippings over medium heat, stirring frequently, until lightly toasted. Add the walnuts, blue cheese, and dried sage to a bowl; mix well. Transfer the mixture into a zippered plastic bag and cut the corner off to create a piping bag. Cut a small slit in the apricots; fill each apricot with the blue cheese mixture. Wrap 1 piece of bacon around each apricot and secure with a toothpick. Place on a rimmed baking sheet. Bake for 10 minutes. Serve warm.

Makes 36

Bacon-Wrapped
Stuffed Apricots

Spicy Smoked Gouda Spread

- 2 cups finely shredded smoked Gouda cheese
- 1 (*4 ounce*) package cream cheese, softened
- ¼ cup mayo
- 1 jalapeño, finely diced
- ½ teaspoon paprika
- ½ teaspoon chipotle powder
- ¼ teaspoon salt
- ¼ teaspoon black pepper

Stir together all ingredients until thoroughly combined. Refrigerate for at least an hour before serving to allow the flavors to develop. Serve with crackers, veggies, or bread.

Serves 6

Peachy Bacon Dip

- 1 tablespoon butter
- ½ cup thinly sliced Vidalia onion
- 2 strips bacon, chopped
- 1 teaspoon black pepper
- ¼ teaspoon salt
- 1 cup cola
- ¼ cup packed brown sugar
- 2 cups coarsely chopped fresh peaches, (*about 3 to 4 peaches*)
- ½ cup chopped pecans
- 2 (*8 ounce*) packages cream cheese, softened

Melt the butter in a large skillet on medium-high heat. Add onion and bacon; cook and stir 6 to 8 minutes or until bacon is crisp.

Stir black pepper, salt, cola, and brown sugar into skillet. Bring to a boil and immediately reduce heat to low; simmer 15 minutes or until mixture thickens slightly, stirring occasionally. Stir in peaches and pecans; simmer until heated through.

Spread cream cheese on the bottom of a pie plate or dish. Top with the warm peach mixture. Serve with assorted crackers or sliced bread.
Serves 10

Mexican Fiesta Board

The Mexican Fiesta Board not only tastes fresh and flavorful, but the pops of color from the peppers, avocado, and salsa make this a board you'll want to show off!

Cheeses: Manchego, cotija
Charcuterie: cured chorizo, honey ham
Bread & Crackers: corn tortillas, blue corn tortilla chips
Accompaniments: pickled jalapeños, pistachios, dried mango, avocados, radishes, sweet mini bells
Condiments & Dips: Corn Salsa (*recipe below*)
Garnish: Cilantro, lime wedges

1. Put the pickled jalapeños, pistachios, and corn salsa in small bowls and place them on the board.
2. Arrange the Manchego, cotija, chorizo, and honey ham on the board.
3. Slice the corn tortillas in half and place them on the board along with some blue corn tortilla chips.
4. Fill in any remaining gaps with dried mango, sliced avocado, radishes, and sweet mini bells.
5. Garnish with cilantro and lime wedges.

Corn Salsa

- 1 (*12 ounce*) bag corn (*thawed & drained*)
- 2 seeded and chopped jalapeños
- ½ cup finely chopped red onion
- ½ cup chopped cilantro
- 1 clove minced garlic
- ½ teaspoon salt
- ½ teaspoon black pepper
- Juice of 2 limes

Combine and serve with tortilla chips.
Makes 2 cups

Tip:
Sprinkle the sliced avocado with lime juice to keep it from turning brown.

Corn Salsa

Mexican Street Corn Dip (Esquites)

- 2 (*8 ounce*) packages cream cheese, softened
- ½ cup sour cream
- 2 garlic cloves, minced
- 2 tablespoons hot sauce, plus more for garnish
- ½ teaspoon paprika
- Juice of 1 lime
- 2 cups shredded Pepper Jack cheese, divided
- 2 (*15 ounce*) cans corn, drained & rinsed
- ½ cup crumbled cotija cheese, plus more for garnish
- 1 jalapeño, seeds removed & diced
- 2 tablespoons chopped red onion
- ½ cup chopped fresh cilantro, plus more for garnish

Preheat oven to 350°.

Combine cream cheese, sour cream, garlic, hot sauce, paprika, lime juice, and 1 cup of the shredded cheese with an electric mixer. Blend until fully combined. Scoop the cream cheese mixture into a large bowl and add the remaining 1 cup Pepper Jack, corn, cotija, jalapeño, onion, and cilantro. Stir to combine.

Pour mixture into a greased baking dish. Bake for 15 to 20 minutes or until cheese is hot and bubbly. Garnish with more cilantro, cotija, and hot sauce. Serve with chips and enjoy!

Serves 8

Holy Guacamole

- 3 ripe avocados
- 1 tablespoon lime juice
- ½ teaspoon salt
- ½ teaspoon ground cumin
- ¼ teaspoon cayenne pepper
- 1 tablespoon chopped fresh cilantro
- 2 tablespoons finely chopped red onion
- 2 Roma tomatoes (*seeded & diced*)
- ½ jalapeño pepper (*seeded & finely chopped*)
- ½ teaspoon minced garlic
- Dash of black pepper

Peel, pit, and dice the avocados and toss into a bowl with lime juice; mash with a fork to reach the desired consistency (*chunky or creamy–your call*). Stir in salt, cumin, cayenne pepper, cilantro, red onion, tomatoes, jalapeño pepper, and garlic. Transfer to a serving bowl and sprinkle with a little black pepper. Serve with tortilla chips or veggies.
Makes about 2 cups

Mango-Peach Salsa

- 1 diced mango
- 1 diced peach
- ¼ cup chopped fresh cilantro
- 1 jalapeño, finely diced
- ½ red bell pepper, diced
- ½ red onion, diced
- 1 tablespoon lemon juice
- 2 tablespoons lime juice
- 1 diced avocado
- 1 teaspoon sea salt
- ½ teaspoon black pepper

In a mixing bowl, stir together the mango, peach, cilantro, jalapeño, red bell pepper, onion, lemon juice, and lime juice. Add the avocado, salt, and black pepper and gently stir to combine. Serve with **Chili-Lime Chips**.
Serves 6

Chili-Lime Chips

Chili-Lime Chips

- 10 corn tortillas
- 2 tablespoons olive oil
- 3 tablespoons lime juice, divided
- 2 teaspoons chili powder
- 1 teaspoon salt

Preheat oven to 350°. Stack the corn tortillas and cut into 6 wedges. Lay the tortilla wedges on a baking sheet.

In a bowl, combine olive oil, 2 tablespoons of lime juice, and chili powder together. Brush the oil mixture onto the tops of the corn tortilla triangles. Flip the triangles and brush the other sides. Bake for 10 to 12 minutes or until chips are firm and lightly browned. Let cool. Sprinkle with remaining 1 tablespoon of lime juice and salt before serving.
Makes 60 chips

Spice It Up Board

This board is perfect for the fans of all things spicy. From ghost pepper Monterey Jack to jalapeño-stuffed olives, you might want to keep a cool pitcher of water on the table—just in case!

Cheeses: ghost pepper Monterey Jack, chipotle queso fresco, honey goat cheese
Charcuterie: peppered salami, cured chorizo
Bread & Crackers: crackers, sliced baguette
Accompaniments: jalapeño-stuffed olives, cherry peppers, green grapes, Bacon & Pepper Almond Brittle (*recipe page 45*), dried apricots, pistachios
Condiments & Dips: Chili Olive Oil (*recipe below*)
Garnish: parsley

1. Put the jalapeño-stuffed olives, cherry peppers, and Chili Olive Oil in small bowls and place them on the board.
2. Arrange the ghost pepper Monterey Jack, chipotle queso fresco, honey goat cheese, peppered salami, and chorizo on the board.
3. Nestle in a few stacks of crackers and baguette slices.
4. Fill in any remaining gaps on the board with green grapes, Bacon & Pepper Almond Brittle, dried apricots, and pistachios.
5. Garnish with fresh parsley and serve.

Chili Olive Oil

- 3 tablespoons crushed red pepper
- ½ teaspoon minced garlic
- 1¼ cup olive oil

Combine crushed red pepper and garlic in a bowl or jar. In a small saucepan, heat olive oil over low heat for 5 minutes. Remove the pan from the heat and carefully pour the oil over the red pepper mixture, making sure the oil completely covers the mixture. Set the oil aside to cool for at least an hour. Depending on your preference, you can either strain out the red pepper or leave it in for added flavor. Store the oil in an airtight container at room temperature for up to 1 month.
Makes 1¼ cups

Chili Olive Oil

Bacon & Pepper
Almond Brittle,
page 45

Jalapeño Popper Dip

- 10 strips bacon
- 1 (*8 ounce*) package cream cheese, softened
- ⅓ cup mayo
- ⅓ cup sour cream
- 1 teaspoon garlic powder
- 1 teaspoon dried minced onion
- 2 jalapeños, minced, divided
- 1½ cups shredded cheddar cheese
- 1½ cups shredded Monterey Jack cheese
- ½ teaspoon seasoned salt
- ¼ teaspoon black pepper

Preheat oven to 350°. In a skillet over medium heat, cook bacon until crispy, about 8 minutes; drain and chop.

Stir together the cream cheese, mayo, sour cream, garlic powder, minced onion, bacon *(reserve some for topping)*, jalapeños *(reserve some for topping)*, and 1 cup each of cheddar and Monterey Jack. Sprinkle with seasoned salt and black pepper.

Transfer to a small oven-safe skillet or baking dish and sprinkle with remaining cheese, bacon, and jalapeño. Bake until golden and bubbly, about 15 to 20 minutes. Serve with crackers.
Serves 8

Chimichurri Dip

- 2 garlic cloves, minced
- 1½ cups chopped fresh parsley
- 2 tablespoons chopped fresh cilantro
- 5 large fresh basil leaves, chopped
- ½ cup olive oil
- 1 tablespoon lime juice
- ½ teaspoon red pepper flakes
- Salt to taste
- Black pepper to taste

Stir garlic and herbs together in a small bowl. Add the olive oil, lime juice, and red pepper flakes; stir well. Season with salt and black pepper. Serve with bread for dipping.
Serves 6

Tip:
This dip is also delicious drizzled on top of grilled steak or chicken.

Hot Pimento Cheese Dip

- 8 ounces shredded sharp cheddar cheese
- 8 ounces shredded Monterey Jack cheese
- 4 ounces pimentos
- 1 jalapeño, diced
- ¼ cup diced green onions
- 1 teaspoon ground cumin
- ½ cup mayo
- 1 (*4 ounce*) package cream cheese, softened

Preheat oven to 350°.
Mix cheddar, Monterey Jack, pimentos, jalapeño, green onions, and cumin. Stir in the mayo and cream cheese until well combined. Spread the mixture evenly into a small skillet. Bake for 20 minutes or until hot and bubbly. Serve with toasted bread, crackers, and veggies.
Serves 8

Bacon & Pepper Almond Brittle

- 6 bacon strips
- 1 cup brown sugar
- ¼ cup butter
- 2 teaspoons salt
- ½ teaspoon coarse-ground black pepper
- 1½ cups unsalted almonds

1. Preheat the oven to 350° and grease a rimmed baking sheet with cooking spray.
2. Cook the bacon until crisp; drain and set aside to cool. Once cooled, crumble into small pieces.
3. In a small saucepan over medium heat, combine the brown sugar, butter, salt, and coarse-ground black pepper; stir until the sugar is dissolved and the mixture begins to bubble.
4. Add the almonds and the crumbled bacon to the saucepan; stir until coated and spread on greased baking sheet. Bake 16 to 18 minutes.
5. Remove from the oven and allow to cool before breaking the brittle apart into bite-sized pieces. Store in an airtight container in the refrigerator for up to 2 weeks.

Serves 8

Spanish Tapas Board

If you love tapas, this board is the perfect way to recreate the experience at home—delicious Spanish queen olives and Manchego cheese is a combination you will want to try.

Cheeses: Manchego, Mahón
Charcuterie: cured chorizo, prosciutto
Bread & Crackers: French bread
Accompaniments: Spanish queen olives, almonds, green grapes, dried figs, pine nuts
Condiments & Dips: Tomato & Goat Cheese Dip *(recipe below)*
Garnish: parsley

1) Put the Spanish queen olives in a small bowl and place them on the board. Place the Tomato & Goat Cheese Dip beside the board.

2) Arrange the Manchego, Mahón, cured chorizo, and prosciutto on the board.

3) Slice a loaf of French bread; cut each slice into quarters and place them on the board.

4) Fill in any remaining gaps with almonds, green grapes, dried figs, and pine nuts.

5) Garnish with parsley and serve.

Tomato & Goat Cheese Dip

- 1 cup canned fire-roasted tomatoes
- 3 cloves minced garlic
- 1 teaspoon sugar
- ½ teaspoon crushed red pepper
- ½ teaspoon black pepper
- ¼ teaspoon salt
- ½ teaspoon paprika
- 4 ounces fresh goat cheese
- Fresh parsley

Preheat the broiler. In a small bowl, combine tomatoes, garlic, sugar, crushed red pepper, black pepper, salt, and paprika. Transfer to an oven-safe dish. Slice goat cheese and dollop over the top of the sauce. Place under the broiler and cook for about 5 minutes or until the cheese bubbles. Garnish with fresh parsley.
Serves 4

Tomato & Goat Cheese Dip

Outrageous Olive Dip

- 1 (*8 ounce*) package cream cheese, softened
- ½ cup mayo
- 1½ cups shredded cheddar cheese
- 1 garlic clove, minced
- ½ cup coarsely chopped pimento stuffed green olives
- ¼ cup chopped fresh parsley

Mix the cream cheese and mayo with an electric mixer until well combined. Add the cheese, garlic, olives, and parsley. Stir to combine. Cover and refrigerate for at least 2 hours before serving. Serve with chips, veggies, or crackers.

Makes about 2½ cups

Creamy Balsamic Bruschetta

- 1 (*8 ounce*) package cream cheese , softened
- ½ teaspoon garlic salt
- 1 teaspoon dried parsley
- ¾ teaspoon black pepper , divided
- 4 diced Roma tomatoes
- ¼ cup diced red onion
- 1 minced garlic clove
- 8 thinly sliced basil leaves , plus more for garnish
- 2 teaspoons balsamic vinegar
- 1 teaspoon olive oil
- ¼ teaspoon salt

Combine cream cheese, garlic salt, dried parsley, and ½ teaspoon black pepper in a small bowl; mix thoroughly. Spread evenly onto a plate or small serving platter. Refrigerate until ready to use.

In a separate bowl, combine tomatoes, onion, garlic, basil, balsamic vinegar, olive oil, salt, and remaining ¼ teaspoon of black pepper. Cover and refrigerate for at least 30 minutes to allow the flavors to develop. When ready to serve, spread the bruschetta over the top of the cream cheese mixture. Garnish with extra basil and serve with crackers or slices of toasted baguette.

Serves 6

Bruschetta Board

The Bruschetta Board provides all the flavors that you love in bruschetta, and makes them an interactive experience. Pile ingredients onto toasted baguette slices or eat them individually, and let the fresh, warm flavors take you to Italy.

Cheeses: fresh mozzarella, aged Asiago
Charcuterie: Genoa salami
Bread & Crackers: Toasted Baguette Slices (*recipe below*)
Accompaniments: Kalamata olives, green grapes, grape tomatoes, almonds
Condiments & Dips: Basil Bruschetta (*recipe below*), honey
Garnish: basil

1 Put the Kalamata olives, Basil Bruschetta, and honey in bowls and place them around the board

2 Arrange the mozzarella, Asiago, and Genoa salami on the board.

3 Add a few stacks of toasted baguette or fill a bread bowl and place it next to the board.

4 Fill in any remaining gaps with green grapes, grape tomatoes, and almonds.

5 Garnish with fresh basil and serve.

Basil Bruschetta

- 2½ cups chopped tomatoes
- 2 minced garlic cloves
- 2 tablespoons olive oil
- 1 tablespoon balsamic vinegar
- 1 teaspoon honey
- 8 finely chopped basil leaves
- Salt & pepper, to taste

Tip:
Basil Bruschetta can be made up to 1 day ahead of time.

In a medium bowl, combine ingredients. Season to taste with salt and pepper. Makes 2½ cups.

Serve with Toasted Baguette Slices: preheat oven to 350°. Slice a baguette loaf into ½" slices. Brush each slice with olive oil and sprinkle with salt. Bake for 10 minutes or until slightly golden.

Basil Bruschetta

Toasted Baguette Slices

Customized Crostini Board

The Customized Crostini Board invites you to recreate your favorite Italian flavors with the perfect crunchy bite! Spread some soft Havarti and Strawberry Bruschetta onto a toasted baguette for a moment of bliss.

Cheeses: Garlic & Herb Boursin, blue cheese, Havarti
Charcuterie: prosciutto, Genoa salami
Bread & Crackers: toasted baguette slices
Accompaniments: marinated olives, arugula, almonds, golden raisins
Condiments & Dips: Strawberry Bruschetta (*recipe below*), Caramelized Onion Jam (*recipe below*), fig jam
Garnish: basil

1. Put the olives, Strawberry Bruschetta, Caramelized Onion Jam, and fig jam in bowls and place them on the board.
2. Arrange the Garlic & Herb Boursin, blue cheese, Havarti, prosciutto, and Genoa salami on the board.
3. Add some toasted baguette slices to the board.
4. Fill in any remaining gaps with arugula, almonds, and golden raisins.
5. Garnish with fresh basil and serve.

Caramelized Onion Jam

- 3 tablespoons olive oil
- 3 thinly sliced white onions
- 2 teaspoons minced garlic
- 2 tablespoons whole grain mustard
- ¼ cup brown sugar
- 2 tablespoons honey
- ¼ cup balsamic vinegar
- 2 cups beef broth
- ¼ teaspoon dried thyme
- ¼ teaspoon black pepper
- ¼ teaspoon salt

Pour olive oil into the bottom of a heavy pot over medium heat. Add onions and garlic; cook uncovered for 10 minutes, stirring every few minutes.
Add mustard, brown sugar, honey, balsamic vinegar, beef broth, thyme, pepper, salt; stir to combine. Cover the pot, lower the heat slightly, and let the mixture simmer for 30 minutes.
Uncover the pot, stir, and cook until most of the liquid is gone and the onions reach a jam-like consistency, approximately 50 minutes. Serve hot or cold with crackers or bread.
Makes about 1 cup

Strawberry Bruschetta

- 1½ cups sliced fresh strawberries,
- 1 diced peach
- 1 cup diced cherry tomatoes
- ¼ cup thinly sliced fresh basil
- 1 diced shallot
- 1 tablespoon olive oil
- 2 tablespoons balsamic vinegar
- 1 teaspoon black pepper
- ¼ teaspoon salt
- 1 (*4 ounce*) package goat cheese

Stir together first nine ingredients. Crumble goat cheese into small pieces and add to the bruschetta mixture; gently fold to combine. Serve with toasted baguette or crackers.
Makes about 3 cups

Caramelized
Onion Jam

Strawberry
Bruschetta

Little Italy Board

Not only do the flavors of the Little Italy Board bring Italy to mind, but the colors look just like the Italian flag! Delicious, fresh meat, rich cheeses, and the pop of cherry tomatoes make this a board to remember.

Cheeses: Marinated Mozzarella Pearls (*recipe below*), aged Asiago, provolone
Charcuterie: mortadella, capicola, soppressata salami
Bread & Crackers: focaccia crackers, sliced baguette
Accompaniments: Castelvetrano olives, pistachios, green grapes, grape tomatoes
Condiments & Dips: fig jam
Garnish: basil

1) Put the Marinated Mozzarella Pearls, Castelvetrano olives, and fig jam in small bowls and place them on the board.

2) Arrange the aged Asiago, provolone, mortadella, capicola, and soppressata salami on the board.

3) Nestle in a few stacks of focaccia crackers and baguette slices.

4) Fill in any remaining gaps on the board with pistachios, green grapes, and grape tomatoes.

5) Garnish with fresh basil and serve.

Marinated Mozzarella Pearls

- ¾ cup olive oil
- 2 cloves minced garlic
- 2 tablespoons finely chopped fresh basil
- 1 tablespoon dried oregano
- ½ teaspoon crushed red pepper
- ¼ teaspoon salt
- ¼ teaspoon black pepper.
- 1 (*8 ounce*) package mozzarella pearls

Mix first seven ingredients. Add mozzarella pearls and stir to coat. Let marinate for at least an hour. The longer they marinate, the stronger the flavor will be. Refrigerate in an airtight container for up to 5 days.

Makes about 40 pearls

Tip:
For a unique presentation, buy a thick slice of mortadella and cube it at home.

Marinated Mozzarella Pearls

Zesty Caesar Dip

- 1 (*8 ounce*) package cream cheese, softened
- 1 cup Caesar salad dressing, plus more for garnish
- ½ cup grated Parmesan cheese, divided
- ¼ teaspoon salt
- ¼ teaspoon black pepper
- 1¼ cups cubed chicken breast, cooked
- 2 cups chopped romaine lettuce
- ½ cup chopped croutons

Beat the cream cheese, salad dressing, ¼ cup of Parmesan, salt, and black pepper with an electric mixer until fully incorporated. Spread the mixture in the bottom of a 9-in. dish.

Top the cream cheese mixture with the chicken and lettuce. Sprinkle with the remaining Parmesan and croutons, then drizzle with a little Caesar salad dressing. Serve with **Baguette Garlic Toast**.
Serves 8

Baguette Garlic Toast

Baguette Garlic Toast

Preheat the oven to 375°. Slice a baguette loaf into ½"-thick pieces and lay in a single layer on a baking sheet. Cut a clove of garlic in half and rub the cut side on each piece of bread. Brush the bread with olive oil and bake for 10 minutes or until crispy. Let cool slightly.
Makes about 20 slices

Supreme Italian Sub Dip

- 1 medium onion
- 2 pickled banana peppers
- ½ head iceberg lettuce
- 1 big tomato (*seeded*)
- 1 (*3 ounce*) package thinly sliced Genoa salami
- 1 (*7 ounce*) package thinly sliced deli ham
- 1 (*7 ounce*) package thinly sliced roasted turkey breast
- ¼ pound thinly sliced white cheddar cheese
- ½ cup mayo
- 1 tablespoon olive oil
- 1 teaspoon dried oregano
- 1½ teaspoons dried basil
- ¼ teaspoon red pepper flakes

Chop first eight ingredients and toss into a bowl.

In a separate bowl, whisk together mayo, olive oil, oregano, basil, and red pepper flakes; add the mixture to the meat and veggies, stirring until combined. Chill until ready to serve.

Carve out the center of a round bread loaf (*we used ciabatta*), keeping the sides and bottom intact. Pack the dip into the hollowed-out bread. Cut the ciabatta bread scraps and 8 hoagie rolls into bite-sized chunks to use for dipping.

Serves 8

Italian Butter Board

Your guests will love digging—or dipping—into this Italian Butter Board. Salty prosciutto, rich Balsamic Glaze, and decadent butter? Yes, please!

- 2 cups of salted butter, softened at room temperature
- ¼ cup fresh basil, chopped, and 10-12 basil leaves for garnish
- 1 (*4-ounce*) package of thinly sliced prosciutto
- ½ cup fig preserves
- 2 ounces pine nuts, toasted
- 1-2 tablespoons balsamic glaze (*recipe below*)
- 2 crusty loaves of bread cut into bite size pieces (*French baguette, sourdough, multi-grain*)

1. Add pine nuts to a small saucepan on low-medium heat. Continuously stir for 2-3 minutes until they become light in color. Do not walk away as they can burn easily. Set aside.

2. Let butter sit out at room temperature overnight. Do not microwave. Butter should be softened, not melted. Add butter to a medium-sized mixing bowl.

3. Chop fresh basil finely. Add to butter and mix thoroughly. (*If not using the butter immediately, cover and chill in the fridge until ready to use, up to 12 hours. Let butter sit out at room temperature for several hours prior to use.*)

4. Spread butter on to wooden board leaving a 2–3-inch border on each side. (*You may spread butter onto cut-to-size parchment paper on the board for easier clean-up.*)

5. Top butter with thin layer of fig preserves.

6. Arrange sliced prosciutto on top. Tear prosciutto for bite-sized pieces.

7. Top with toasted cooled pine nuts.

8. Drizzle balsamic glaze on top of butter.

9. Sprinkle basil leaves on top of butter.

10. Arrange bread along the borders of the board for dipping.

Serves 6–8

Balsamic Glaze

- ½ cup balsamic vinegar
- ¼ cup honey
- ¼ teaspoon garlic salt

Balsamic Glaze: Combine balsamic vinegar, honey, and garlic salt in a small saucepan over medium heat. Cook and stir until the mixture begins to foam. Reduce heat to low and simmer, stirring occasionally, for 10 minutes.

Balsamic Glaze

Antipasto Board

This Antipasto Board doesn't have to just be served before the meal—it's delicious and filling enough to be the meal itself! The Marinated Antipasto Skewers are a fun addition, too; colorful, interesting, and portable.

Cheeses: Parmigiano-Reggiano, fresh mozzarella
Charcuterie: mortadella, capicola, soppressata salami
Bread & Crackers: cubed French bread
Accompaniments: marinated olives, marinated artichoke hearts, pepperoncini peppers, grape tomatoes, almonds, Marinated Antipasto Skewers (*recipe page 62*)
Dips & Condiments: Garlic Dipping Oil (*recipe below*)
Garnish: basil

1. Put the olives, artichoke hearts, pepperoncini peppers, and Garlic Dipping Oil in small bowls and place them on the board.
2. Arrange the Parmigiano-Reggiano, mozzarella, mortadella, capicola, and soppressata salami on the board.
3. Add a few piles of cubed French bread.
4. Fill in any remaining gaps with grape tomatoes, almonds, and Marinated Antipasto Skewers.
5. Garnish with fresh basil and serve.

Garlic Dipping Oil

- 1 cup extra virgin olive oil
- 1 clove minced garlic
- ¼ cup balsamic vinegar,
- ¼ teaspoon salt
- Black pepper to taste

Pour olive oil into a small pan and set over medium-low heat. Add garlic and heat until just warmed. Pour the olive oil into a shallow bowl. Immediately add balsamic vinegar, salt, pepper.
Makes 1½ cups

Garlic Dipping Oil

Marinated Antipasto Skewers

- 🥄 1 (*9 ounce*) package tortellini
- 🥄 1 (*8 ounce*) package mozzarella pearls
- 🥄 1 cup Italian dressing
- 🥄 ½ teaspoon black pepper
- 🥄 ¼ teaspoon Italian seasoning
- 🥄 1 teaspoon dried parsley
- 🥄 40 Kalamata olives
- 🥄 40 spinach leaves
- 🥄 40 pepperoni slices

1. Cook the tortellini according to package directions; drain and rinse.
2. Add the tortellini to a mixing bowl along with the mozzarella pearls, Italian dressing, black pepper, Italian seasoning, and dried parsley. Gently stir to combine, cover, and refrigerate for at least 2 hours, stirring halfway through.
3. To assemble, thread one tortellini, mozzarella pearl, olive, spinach leaf, and pepperoni slice onto a small wooden skewer, folding the pepperoni and spinach leaves in quarters before skewering.

Makes 40

Zippy Pepperoncini Spread

- 1 (*8 ounce*) package cream cheese, softened
- ½ cup crumbled feta cheese
- 2 tablespoons olive oil
- 1 tablespoon juice from jar of pepperoncini peppers
- ½ teaspoon black pepper
- ½ teaspoon red pepper flakes
- 1 garlic clove, minced
- ½ cup chopped pepperoncini peppers
- 1 tablespoon chopped fresh chives

Beat cream cheese, feta cheese, oil, pepperoncini juice, black pepper, red pepper flakes, and garlic with an electric mixer until smooth. Add the peppers and chives and mix until completely incorporated. Chill before serving to allow the flavors to develop. Serve with crackers.

Makes 2 cups

French Classics Board

This board has all the flavors of your favorite French dishes, so you don't have to pick and choose. But be warned that the Raspberry Brie Crescents are dangerous—you can't have just one!

Cheeses: Camembert, Roquefort blue cheese
Charcuterie: jambon de Paris
Bread & Crackers: sliced baguette
Accompaniments: cornichons, hazelnuts, golden raisins, dried apricots, Raspberry Brie Crescents (*recipe below*)
Condiments & Dips: Dijon mustard, honey
Garnish: thyme

1. Put the cornichons, Dijon mustard, and honey in small bowls and place them on the board.
2. Arrange the Camembert, Roquefort blue cheese, and jambon de Paris on the board.
3. Nestle in a few baguette slices.
4. Fill in any remaining gaps on the board with hazelnuts, golden raisins, dried apricots, and Raspberry Brie Crescents.
5. Garnish with fresh thyme and serve.

Raspberry Brie Crescents

- 1 (*8 ounce*) tube crescent roll dough
- 1 (*8 ounce*) wheel of Brie cheese
- Raspberry preserves to taste
- Dried thyme to taste

Preheat the oven to 375° and grease a mini muffin tin with cooking spray. On a lightly floured surface, unroll the crescent roll dough and pinch together the seams. Cut into 24 rectangles. Press the rectangles into the muffin tin. Cut Brie cheese into small pieces and place 1 piece inside each dough-lined muffin tin. Top the Brie with a dollop of raspberry preserves and a pinch of dried thyme. Bake for 15 minutes or until the crescent dough is golden brown and the cheese is melted.
Makes 24

Raspberry Brie
Crescents

Molten Brie & Onion Dip

- 2 tablespoons olive oil
- 1 thinly sliced yellow onion
- ¼ cup apple cider
- 2 (*8 ounce*) wheels of Brie cheese
- Salt and pepper to taste
- Fresh chives to taste

Heat olive oil in a skillet over medium heat. Add onion and reduce the heat to low. Allow the onions to caramelize slowly, stirring occasionally until they are a deep golden brown. Once the onions are caramelized, deglaze the pan with apple cider. Scrape up any stuck-on pieces and stir into the onions.

Remove the rind from the Brie cheese and cut into small chunks. Turn off the heat and stir in the brie cheese until melted. Season with salt and pepper to taste. Transfer to a serving dish and sprinkle fresh chives on top. Serve with bread and crackers.

Serves 8

Mustard Pretzel Dip

- 1 cup sour cream
- 1 cup mayo
- 1 cup yellow mustard
- 1 tablespoon sugar
- 1 tablespoon dried minced onion
- 1 package ranch seasoning
- 1 teaspoon paprika
- 1 tablespoon prepared horseradish

Combine all ingredients and stir until well combined. Cover and refrigerate for at least 30 minutes to allow the flavors to develop. Serve with pretzels, veggies, or crackers.

Makes 3 cups

Classic German Board

The Classic German Board showcases delicious sausages, tangy pickles, and light, sweet German Raspberry Mustard. This board is filling, colorful, and memorable.

Cheeses: Gouda, caraway cheddar
Charcuterie: Braunschweiger, summer sausage, grilled bratwurst
Bread & Crackers: rye chips, pretzel chips, pretzel bread
Accompaniments: sweet gherkins, green grapes, hazelnuts
Condiments & Dips: German Raspberry Mustard *(recipe below)*
Garnish: parsley

1 Put the sweet gherkins and German Raspberry Mustard in small bowls and place them on the board.

2 Arrange the Gouda, caraway cheddar, Braunschweiger, summer sausage, and bratwurst on the board.

3 Nestle in some rye chips and pretzel chips. Slice a loaf of pretzel bread and place it next to the board.

4 Fill in any remaining gaps with green grapes and hazelnuts.

5 Garnish with fresh parsley and serve.

German Raspberry Mustard

- 2 tablespoons brown sugar
- 1 tablespoon balsamic vinegar
- ½ pint fresh raspberries
- 1 tablespoon dry mustard
- 1 tablespoon mustard seeds
- ¼ teaspoon salt
- ¼ teaspoon black pepper

Tip:
Braunschweiger can be served in slices or spread on crackers.

In a small saucepan, mix brown sugar and balsamic vinegar; cook over medium heat until the sugar dissolves. Reduce the heat to low and add raspberries; cook 10 minutes more. Add dry mustard, mustard seeds, salt, and black pepper; cook 10 minutes more.
Makes 1 cup

German Raspberry Mustard

Reuben Dip

- 1 (*8 ounce*) package cream cheese, softened
- ½ cup sour cream
- ½ cup Thousand Island dressing
- 1 (*14.5 ounce*) can sauerkraut (*drained*)
- 1 cup chopped corned beef
- 1 cup shredded Swiss cheese, divided
- ¼ cup chopped green onions, plus more for garnish

Preheat oven to 350°. In a mixing bowl, stir together the cream cheese, sour cream, and Thousand Island dressing until combined. Add the sauerkraut, corned beef, ½ cup cheese, and green onions; stir to combine. Transfer to an oven-safe baking dish and top with the remaining ½ cup cheese. Bake until bubbly and golden, about 20 minutes. Garnish with green onions before serving. Serve with toasted marble rye bread.

Slow cooker instructions: transfer the dip mixture into a slow cooker and cook on low for about 2 hours, stirring occasionally.

Serves 8

The unbaked dip can be refrigerated overnight.

BLT Dip

- 1 (*8 ounce*) package cream cheese, softened
- ¾ cup mayo
- 2 tablespoons ranch seasoning
- ¾ cup finely shredded romaine lettuce
- 1 cup diced tomatoes, seeded
- 5 strips bacon, cooked & crumbled
- ¼ cup sliced green onions

Beat the cream cheese with an electric mixer until smooth. Add the mayo and ranch seasoning and beat until fully combined.

Spread the ranch mixture into the bottom of a plate or dish. Top the ranch mixture with lettuce, tomatoes, bacon and sliced green onions. Serve with crackers or toasted bread.

Serves 8

All-American Board

This board has the perfect balance of crunchy and soft, salty and sweet, and effortless and thoughtful. The Overnight Bread & Butter Pickles will have your guests asking for more, so be sure to come prepared!

Cheeses: Pepper Jack, cheese curds, Maytag blue cheese
Charcuterie: mesquite-smoked turkey, summer sausage, Black Forest ham
Bread & Crackers: woven wheat crackers
Accompaniments: Overnight Bread & Butter Pickles *(recipe below)*, raspberries, pecans, almonds, dried cranberries, honey-roasted peanuts
Condiments & Dips: raspberry preserves, honey mustard
Garnish: parsley

1. Put the Overnight Bread & Butter Pickles, raspberry preserves, and honey mustard in small bowls and place them on the board.
2. Arrange the Pepper Jack, cheese curds, Maytag blue cheese, mesquite-smoked turkey, summer sausage, and Black Forest ham on the board
3. Nestle in a pile of woven wheat crackers.
4. Fill in any remaining gaps with raspberries, pecans, almonds, dried cranberries, and honey-roasted peanuts.
5. Garnish with fresh parsley and serve.

Overnight Bread & Butter Pickles

- 4 mini cucumbers, sliced
- 3 tablespoons kosher salt
- ½ cup sugar
- ¼ cup brown sugar
- 1 cup apple cider vinegar
- 2 teaspoons mustard seed

Place the sliced cucumbers in a bowl. Toss with salt and chill in the refrigerator for 1 hour. Remove from the fridge and rinse with cold water. Drain and place the cucumbers in a pint jar. Combine sugar, brown sugar, apple cider vinegar, and mustard seed in a saucepan over medium heat. Simmer until the sugar is dissolved. Remove from the heat and pour over the cucumbers. Let cool at room temperature for 30 minutes then seal and chill in the refrigerator overnight before serving. Store in the refrigerator for up to 3 weeks.

Makes 1 pint

Overnight Bread & Butter Pickles

Sizzlin' Buffalo Ranch Dip

- 1 *(8 ounce)* package cream cheese
- ½ cup buffalo-style hot sauce
- ½ cup sour cream
- ¼ cup ranch dressing
- 1 cup cooked chicken
- 1½ cups shredded Monterey Jack cheese
- ¼ cup finely sliced green onions
- ½ cup shredded Monterey Jack cheese

Preheat the oven to 375°. In a large bowl, mix cream cheese, hot sauce, sour cream, and ranch dressing until combined. Stir in chicken, 1½ cups of shredded Monterey Jack cheese, and green onions. Scrape the mixture into a medium cast-iron skillet or oven- safe dish and sprinkle ½ cups of shredded Monterey jack cheese on top.

Bake the dip for 20 minutes, until bubbling. Turn on the broiler and broil 6 inches from the heat until lightly browned on top. Let cool for 5 minutes before garnishing with green onions. Serve with chips, crackers, or veggies. The unbaked dip can be refrigerated overnight. Let stand at room temperature for 20 minutes before baking.

Serves 8

Loaded Baked Potato Dip

- 8 strips bacon, cooked & crumbled
- 2 cups sour cream
- ¼ cup finely chopped green onions
- 1 cup shredded sharp cheddar cheese
- 2 garlic cloves, minced
- 1 teaspoon dried minced onion
- ¼ teaspoon seasoned salt
- 1 teaspoon black pepper

Combine all ingredients in a large mixing bowl. Chill for at least one hour before serving to allow the flavors to develop. Transfer to a serving bowl and serve with potato chips.

Serves a crowd
This will become your go-to potato chip dip!

Budget Board

Board building doesn't have to break the bank! The items found on the Budget Board might even be in your pantry right now—placing them together to balance all of the delicious flavors is what will make your board shine.

Cheeses: Colby-Jack, Swiss
Charcuterie: Black Forest ham, pepperoni, beef sticks
Bread & Crackers: butter crackers
Accompaniments: sweet gherkins, Crispy Chickpeas *(recipe below)*, pears, dried cranberries, almonds, arugula
Condiments & Dips: peach preserves

1 Put the sweet gherkins, Crispy Chickpeas, and peach preserves in small bowls and place them on the board.

2 Arrange the Colby-Jack, Swiss, Black Forest ham, pepperoni, and beef sticks on the board.

3 Nestle in a stack of butter crackers.

4 Fill in any remaining gaps with sliced pears, dried cranberries, almonds, and arugula.

Crispy Chickpeas

- 2 *(15 ounce)* cans of chickpeas
- 2 tablespoon olive oil
- 2 teaspoons salt
- ¼ teaspoon garlic powder
- ½ teaspoon parsley
- ¼ teaspoon black pepper
- ¼ teaspoon paprika

Tip:
Reheat any leftover Crispy Chickpeas in a skillet over medium heat for 5 minutes, stirring often. This will crisp them up again.

Preheat the oven to 400°. Drain and rinse chickpeas. Let air-dry for a few minutes before patting dry with a paper towel. In a large mixing bowl, combine the chickpeas, olive oil, salt, and garlic powder. Spread in a single layer on a rimmed baking sheet. Roast for 50 minutes, turning halfway through. Toss the roasted chickpeas with parsley, black pepper, and paprika. Serve while the chickpeas are slightly warm and crispy.
Makes 2 cups

Crispy Chickpeas

Perfect Pickles Board

Calling all pickle lovers! The briny, tangy pickled vegetables on this board combine beautifully with the creamy cheeses and soft bread. Dig in!

Cheeses: aged cheddar, Maytag blue cheese
Charcuterie: deli roast beef, summer sausage
Bread & Crackers: crackers, French bread
Accompaniments: dill pickle medley, Easy Pickled Asparagus *(recipe below)*, pickled beets, cocktail onions, almonds, sweet gherkins, dried apricots
Condiments & Dips: spicy brown mustard, raspberry preserves
Garnish: dill

1. Put the dill pickle medley, Easy Pickled Asparagus, beets, cocktail onions, spicy brown mustard, and raspberry preserves in dishes and place them on the board.
2. Arrange the aged cheddar, Maytag blue cheese, roast beef, and summer sausage on the board.
3. Add some crackers and sliced French bread.
4. Fill in any remaining gaps with almonds, sweet gherkins, and dried apricots.
5. Garnish with fresh dill and serve.

Easy Pickled Asparagus

- 2 pounds asparagus
- 1½ cups water
- 1 cup apple cider vinegar
- 1½ tablespoons salt
- 1 tablespoon brown sugar
- 4 cloves garlic
- 3 fresh dill sprigs
- 1 teaspoon mustard seed
- ½ teaspoon black peppercorns
- ¼ teaspoon crushed red pepper

Wash and trim the ends off the asparagus. Boil a pot of water and prepare a bowl of ice water. Once the water reaches a boil, drop the asparagus in for 10 seconds. Drain the asparagus and transfer to the ice water.

Bring water, apple cider vinegar, salt, and brown sugar to a boil; remove from the heat and let cool. Meanwhile, place garlic, dill sprigs, mustard seed, black peppercorns, and crushed red pepper into the bottom of a quart jar. Fill with asparagus and top with brine. Seal and place in the refrigerator for at least 2 days before serving. Refrigerate up to 1 month.

Makes 1 quart

Easy Pickled
Asparagus

Double Dill Dip

- 1 (*8 ounce*) package softened cream cheese
- ¼ cup pickle juice
- 1½ cups chopped dill pickles
- 1 cup shredded cheddar cheese
- ¼ teaspoon garlic powder
- ½ teaspoon dried dill
- ½ cups chopped Genoa salami
- ¼ teaspoon black pepper
- ¼ cup diced red onion

Mix cream cheese and pickle juice with an electric mixer until combined. Add dill pickles, cheddar cheese, garlic powder, dill, salami, black pepper, and red onion; stir to combine. Cover and refrigerate for at least 2 hours before serving to allow the flavors to develop. Serve with crackers, pretzels, or veggies.

Makes about 4 cups

Cucumber Cream Cheese

Cube ½ cucumber and slice 3 green onions. Process the cucumbers and onions in a food processor until coarsely chopped. Add 1 (*8 ounce*) package softened cream cheese, 1 teaspoon Worcestershire sauce, ¼ teaspoon garlic powder, ¼ teaspoon salt, and ¼ teaspoon black pepper and process until smooth. Transfer to a bowl and refrigerate for at least 1 hour to allow the flavors to develop. Serve with crackers, pretzels, or veggies.

Makes 1½ cups

Coastal Shrimp Dip

- 2 tablespoons butter
- 1 pound shrimp, peeled, deveined, & coarsely chopped
- 1 garlic clove, minced
- 4 green onions, sliced
- 1 tablespoon lemon juice
- 1 cup mayo
- ¼ cup sour cream
- ½ cup cream cheese, softened
- ¼ cup shredded Parmesan cheese
- ¼ cup minced bell pepper
- 2 tablespoons finely chopped fresh parsley
- ½ teaspoon Old Bay seasoning
- ¼ teaspoon celery salt
- ¼ teaspoon black pepper
- 1 cup mozzarella cheese, shredded

Preheat the oven to 350°. Melt butter in a skillet over medium heat. Add shrimp, garlic, and onions and cook just until the shrimp are pink. Stir in lemon juice and remove from heat.

Combine the shrimp mixture, mayo, sour cream, cream cheese, Parmesan, bell pepper, parsley, Old Bay, celery salt, and black pepper. Transfer to an oven-safe dish and top with mozzarella. Bake until golden and bubbly, about 20 to 25 minutes. Serve with bread or crackers.

Serves 8

Mediterranean Board

The Mediterranean Board brings you fresh vegetables, crunchy breads, and a satisfied feeling. It's filling, yet doesn't weigh you down! Kalamata olives are essential to this board.

Cheeses: feta, Manchego
Charcuterie: soppressata salami
Bread & Crackers: pita chips, flatbread
Accompaniments: marinated artichoke hearts, Kalamata olives, cucumbers, pistachios, grape tomatoes
Condiments & Dips: hummus, Tzatziki Dip (*recipe below*)
Garnish: dill

1. Put the artichoke hearts, olives, hummus, and Tzatziki Dip in small bowls and place them on the board.
2. Arrange the feta, Manchego, and salami on the board.
3. Nestle in some pita chips. Cut each flatbread into quarters and place them alongside the board.
4. Fill in any remaining gaps with cucumbers, pistachios, and grape tomatoes.
5. Garnish with fresh dill and serve.

Tzatziki Dip

- ½ large cucumber
- 1½ cups plain full-fat Greek yogurt
- 1 clove minced garlic
- 2 tablespoons extra virgin olive oil
- 1 tablespoon distilled white vinegar
- ½ teaspoon salt
- ¼ teaspoon black pepper
- 1 tablespoon minced fresh dill

Grate cucumber and squeeze out the excess moisture. Combine the grated cucumber, plain full-fat Greek yogurt, garlic, olive oil, vinegar, salt, black pepper, and dill in a large bowl. Cover and refrigerate for at least 2 hours to allow the flavors to meld. Serve chilled.
Makes 2 cups

Tzatziki Dip

Mediterranean Roasted Garlic Butter Board

The pita bread and olive oil included on this butter board truly gives it a Mediterranean feel. Feel free to scoop with cucumbers or slices of bread, too!

- 2 cups of unsalted butter, softened at room temperature
- 1 large head of garlic
- 2 teaspoons olive oil
- ½ teaspoon fresh oregano, chopped very finely and 10-12 whole oregano leaves for garnish
- ½ teaspoon fresh mint, chopped very finely, and 10-12 whole mint leaves for garnish
- 1 shallot or ½ red onion, sliced very thinly
- 1 (*12-ounce*) jar roasted red peppers, drained well, and sliced in thin strips
- 1 (*6 -ounce*) jar Kalamata olives, drained and sliced in half
- 1 (*5-ounce*) container crumbled feta cheese, or one block of feta cheese, crumbled
- 1 crusty loaf of bread cut into bite size pieces (*French baguette, sourdough, multi-grain*)
- 2 bags pita chips
- 1 bag pita bread, cut into wedges
- 2 thinly sliced English cucumbers, or regular cucumbers, seeds removed

1. Preheat oven to 400°.
2. Peel and discard any loose outer leaves of garlic but do not separate apart. Cut ½ off the top of the garlic bulb to expose the garlic cloves.
3. Drizzle the garlic with olive oil, rubbing to ensure oil goes down into the garlic cloves.
4. Wrap garlic bulb tightly in aluminum foil and place on a baking sheet. Bake in the oven for 35 to 40 minutes until the garlic cloves are lightly browned and very soft. Let cool and set aside.
5. Let butter sit out at room temperature overnight. Do not microwave. Butter should be softened, not melted. Add butter to a medium size mixing bowl.
6. Chop fresh oregano and mint finely. Add to butter and mix thoroughly.
7. Chop and smash roasted garlic and add to the butter mixture. Mix thoroughly. (*If not using the butter immediately, cover and chill in the fridge until ready to use, up to 24 hours. Let butter sit out at room temperature for several hours prior to use.*)
8. Spread butter on to wooden board leaving a 2–3-inch border on each side. (*You may spread butter onto cut-to-size parchment paper on the board for easier clean-up.*)
9. Top butter with thin layer of drained and halved Kalamata olives, thin slices of shallot/onion, red peppers, and crumbled feta cheese.
10. Sprinkle reserved whole oregano and mint leaves all over butter. Arrange pita chips, pita bread, bread, and cucumber slices along the borders of the board for dipping.

Serves 6–8

Veggie Lovers Board

Bright, colorful, and fresh, the Veggie Lovers Board combines fresh vegetables with delicious cheeses and dips. You're sure to hear some happy crunching around the table!

Cheeses: feta, sharp cheddar, Havarti
Bread & Crackers: crackers
Accompaniments: Castelvetrano olives, marinated artichoke hearts, red grapes, cherry tomatoes, arugula, almonds, baby carrots, broccoli florets, sweet mini bells, radishes
Condiments & Dips: Herb & Garlic Dip (*recipe below*), hummus
Garnish: dill

1. Put the Castelvetrano olives, artichoke hearts, Herb & Garlic Dip, and hummus in small bowls and place them on the board.
2. Arrange the feta, sharp cheddar, and Havarti on the board.
3. Nestle in a stack or two of crackers.
4. Fill in any remaining gaps with red grapes, cherry tomatoes, arugula, almonds, baby carrots, broccoli florets, sweet mini bells, and radishes.
5. Garnish with fresh dill and serve.

Herb & Garlic Dip

- 1 cup mayo
- ½ cup sour cream
- 1 tablespoon dried parsley
- 1 tablespoon dried chives
- ½ teaspoon dried tarragon
- 1 teaspoon dried dill
- 1 teaspoon minced garlic
- ½ teaspoon dried minced onion
- ¼ teaspoon paprika
- ¼ teaspoon salt
- ¼ teaspoon black pepper

Combine all ingredients in a mixing bowl. Refrigerate for several hours to allow the flavors to develop. Serve with veggies or crackers.
Makes 1½ cups

Herb & Garlic Dip

Cumin Hummus

- ¼ cup tahini
- ¼ cup lemon juice
- 2 tablespoons olive oil
- 1 minced garlic clove
- ½ teaspoon ground cumin
- ½ teaspoon salt
- 1 (*14 ounce*) can chickpeas (*drained & rinsed*)
- 2 tablespoons water

In the bowl of a food processor, combine tahini and lemon juice and process for 1½ minutes, scraping the sides and bottom of the bowl once. Add olive oil, garlic, cumin, and salt and process for 1 minute, until well blended, scraping the bowl once. Add chickpeas and process for 1 minute; scrape the bowl and continue processing until thick and smooth. With the food processor running, slowly add water through the chute, until the hummus is very smooth. Taste and add extra salt if needed. Transfer to a serving bowl, drizzle with a little oil, sprinkle with paprika, and serve with veggies.

Makes 2 cups

Sesame-Ginger Guac

- 3 ripe avocados
- 1 tablespoon rice vinegar
- 1 tablespoon lime juice
- 1 tablespoon soy sauce
- 1 tablespoon sesame oil
- 2 teaspoons freshly grated ginger
- 2 finely sliced green onions
- ¼ teaspoon red pepper

Peel, pit, and dice avocados and toss into a mixing bowl; mash with a fork. Add rice vinegar, lime juice, soy sauce, sesame oil, ginger, green onions, and red pepper flakes; gently stir to combine. Garnish with sesame seeds and green onions. Serve immediately with tortilla chips, pita chips, or fresh veggies.

Makes about 2 cups

Crab Rangoon Dip

- 1 (*8 ounce*) package cream cheese, softened
- ¼ cup mayo
- ¼ cup sour cream
- 1 cup shredded Monterey Jack cheese, divided
- ¼ cup shredded Parmesan cheese
- 3 green onions, sliced
- 2 tablespoons Worcestershire sauce
- 2 teaspoons soy sauce
- 1 teaspoon Sriracha
- ½ teaspoon garlic powder
- Salt & black pepper to taste
- 12 ounces imitation crab meat

Preheat oven to 350°. Lightly coat a 9-in. baking dish or cast-iron skillet with nonstick spray.

In a large bowl, combine cream cheese, mayo, and sour cream. Stir in ½ cup Monterey Jack cheese, Parmesan, green onions, Worcestershire, soy sauce, Sriracha, garlic powder, and salt and pepper. Fold in the imitation crab meat.

Transfer to the prepared baking dish; top with remaining ½ cup Monterey Jack cheese. Bake until bubbly and golden, about 20 to 25 minutes. Serve with crackers or veggies.

Serves 8

Blueberry-Basil Salsa

- 2 ears raw corn, cut off the cob
- 1 cup blueberries
- ½ red onion, finely diced
- 3 mini sweet peppers, cut into rings
- ½ cup thinly sliced fresh basil
- ¼ teaspoon black pepper
- 1 tablespoon olive oil
- Juice of 1 lime
- Salt to taste

Toss together the raw corn, blueberries, onion, peppers, fresh basil, and black pepper. Drizzle with the olive oil and lime juice and gently stir to combine. Season to taste with salt and serve at room temperature or chilled. Serve with tortilla chips.

Makes about 2 cups

Mediterranean Salsa

- 1 (*10.5 ounce*) can chickpeas (*drained*)
- 1 garlic clove, minced
- ½ cup diced cucumber
- 1 cup diced tomato
- ½ cup diced Kalamata olives
- ¼ cup diced red onion
- 1 tablespoon chopped fresh parsley
- ¼ teaspoon dried oregano
- ½ teaspoon dried dill
- 1 tablespoon chopped fresh basil
- 1 tablespoon lemon juice
- 1 tablespoon extra-virgin olive oil
- ½ teaspoon salt
- ½ teaspoon black pepper

Add all the ingredients to a bowl and toss to combine. Serve immediately or refrigerate until ready to serve. Serve with pita chips or tortilla chips.

Serves 6

Spinach Cheese Puffs

- ½ cup cream cheese
- ½ cup shredded mozzarella
- ¼ cup ricotta cheese
- ¼ cup finely chopped spinach leaves
- 1 clove minced garlic
- 1 teaspoon dried parsley
- 1 teaspoon chopped chives
- ¼ teaspoon salt
- ¼ teaspoon black pepper
- 1 (*14 ounce*) package puff pastry, thawed
- Flour for dusting
- 1 egg

1. In a mixing bowl, combine cream cheese, mozzarella, ricotta, spinach, garlic, parsley, chives, salt, and black pepper.
2. Unfold the pastry sheets on a floured work surface. Cut each sheet into 12 rectangles (*24 total*). Add about 1 teaspoon of filling to each.
3. Whisk together the egg. Brush the edges of each pastry square with egg wash and fold in half. Press the edges with a fork to seal. Place them in the refrigerator to chill for 15 minutes.
4. Preheat the oven to 400°. Bake for 20 to 22 minutes or until golden and puffy.

Makes 24

Spring Greens Board

The Spring Greens Board is light, fresh, and perfect for a summer's day. The Green Goddess Dip is always a crowd pleaser!

Cheeses: blue cheese, Swiss, Brie
Charcuterie: soppressata salami, mortadella
Bread & Crackers: woven wheat crackers
Accompaniments: cocktail onions, sugar snap peas, mini cucumbers, macadamia nuts, Spinach Cheese Puffs (*recipe on page 91*)
Condiments & Dips: Green Goddess Dip (*recipe below*)
Garnish: basil

1. Put the cocktail onions and Green Goddess Dip in small bowls and place them on the board.
2. Arrange the blue cheese, Swiss, Brie, soppressata salami, and mortadella on the board.
3. Fill a bowl with woven wheat crackers and place it alongside the board.
4. Fill in any remaining gaps with sugar snap peas, mini cucumbers, macadamia nuts, and Spinach Cheese Puffs.
5. Garnish with fresh basil and serve.

Green Goddess Dip

- 2 cups packed arugula
- ½ cup fresh basil leaves
- 3 tablespoons chopped fresh chives
- 1 tablespoon chopped fresh parsley
- ½ teaspoon lemon zest
- ½ cup mayo
- ¼ cup sour cream
- 1 teaspoon Dijon mustard
- 2 garlic cloves
- ¼ teaspoon salt
- ¼ teaspoon black pepper

Combine the arugula, basil, chives, parsley, and lemon zest in a food processor; process for 10 seconds. Add the mayo, sour cream, Dijon mustard, garlic, salt, and black pepper. Process until all ingredients are finely chopped. Cover and chill for at least an hour before serving to allow the flavors to develop. Serve with veggies and crackers.

Makes 1½ cups

Green Goddess Dip

5-Cheese Artichoke Dip

This 5-Cheese Artichoke dip is delicious, cheesy, and perfect for guests to dip some crackers or bread in. It's also beautiful, so don't be surprised if people will want to take pictures!

- 1 (*16 ounce*) jar roasted sweet red peppers, drained & chopped
- 1 (*6.5 ounce*) jar marinated quartered artichoke hearts, drained & chopped
- 1 (*10 ounces*) package frozen chopped spinach, thawed & squeezed dry
- 1½ cups shredded Parmesan cheese
- 1 (*8 ounce*) package cream cheese, softened & cubed
- 1 cup crumbled feta cheese
- 1 cup shredded provolone cheese, divided
- ⅓ cup minced fresh basil
- ¼ cup finely chopped red onion
- 2 tablespoons mayo
- 2 garlic cloves, minced
- ½ teaspoon black pepper
- ½ teaspoon salt
- 8 ounces fresh mozzarella cheese, cubed

Mix the peppers, artichokes, spinach, Parmesan, cream cheese, feta, provolone, basil, onion, mayo, garlic, black pepper, and salt in a large mixing bowl. Transfer the mixture to an oven-safe baking dish and top with the cubed mozzarella. Bake until bubbly and golden, about 25 minutes. Serve with crackers or bread.

Serves a crowd

Summer Bounty Board

This board is everything that I love about summer. Fresh, light fruits, crunchy veggies, sweet and salty meats, and mouth-watering Feta & Tomato Dip. What could be more delicious?

Cheeses: aged cheddar, Camembert, Colby-Jack
Charcuterie: summer sausage, honey ham, mesquite-smoked turkey
Bread & Crackers: woven wheat crackers, whole-wheat crackers
Accompaniments: Prosciutto-Wrapped Cantaloupe (*recipe below*), strawberries, peaches, grape tomatoes, mini cucumbers
Condiments & Dips: peach preserves, Feta & Tomato Dip (*recipe on page 98*), balsamic glaze (*recipe on page 58*)
Garnish: basil

1. Put the peach preserves and Feta & Tomato Dip in bowls and place them around the board.
2. Arrange the aged cheddar, Camembert, Colby-Jack, summer sausage, honey ham, and smoked turkey on the board.
3. Nestle in a few stacks of woven wheat and whole-wheat crackers.
4. Fill in any remaining gaps with Prosciutto-Wrapped Cantaloupe, strawberries, sliced peaches, grape tomatoes, and mini cucumbers.
5. Garnish with fresh basil and serve.

PROSCIUTTO-WRAPPED CANTALOUPE

- 1 cantaloupe
- 1 piece prosciutto

Cut a cantaloupe into 1" squares. Cut a piece of prosciutto in half lengthwise and across so it's in four pieces. Wrap a piece of cantaloupe in prosciutto. Place a basil leaf on top and pierce with a toothpick to hold it together. Repeat for each skewer you want to make.

Prosciutto-Wrapped
Cantaloupe

Feta & Tomato Dip,
page 98

Feta & Tomato Dip

- 1½ cups diced Roma tomatoes
- ¼ cup finely chopped green onion
- 8 ounces crumbled feta
- ¼ cup sliced Kalamata olives
- ¼ teaspoon minced garlic
- ¼ teaspoon black pepper
- ¼ teaspoon dried dill
- ¼ teaspoon dried marjoram
- Olive oil
- Balsamic vinegar
- Fresh basil

In a large mixing bowl, gently toss together the tomatoes, green onion, feta, olives, garlic, black pepper, dill, and marjoram. Cover and refrigerate for at least an hour before serving to allow the flavors to develop.

Before serving, spread the dip on a small plate or dish. Finish with a light drizzle of olive oil and balsamic vinegar. Garnish with fresh basil. Serve with crackers, flatbread, or pita chips.

Pesto Hummus

- 2 (*14 ounce*) cans chickpeas, drained and rinsed
- ½ cup fresh basil leaves, plus more for garnish
- ¼ cup grated Parmesan cheese
- ¼ cup olive oil, plus more for garnish
- 1 tablespoon pine nuts, plus more for garnish
- 3 garlic cloves, minced
- Juice of 1 lemon
- ½ teaspoon black pepper
- Salt to taste

Combine all the ingredients except salt in a food processor and blend on high until smooth. Season with salt. Transfer the hummus to a serving dish and refrigerate for at least 30 minutes to allow flavors to develop. Garnish with basil, pine nuts, and a drizzle of olive oil before serving. Serve with **Black Pepper Pita Chips**.

Keep covered in your fridge for up to 5 days.

Serves 8

Black Pepper Pita Chips

Brush olive oil over one side of 5 pita bread rounds; sprinkle with sea salt and coarse black pepper. Cut each round into eight triangles and bake at 375° for 10 minutes or until toasted.

Makes 40

Fresh Watermelon Salsa

- ¼ cup balsamic vinegar
- 1 tablespoon sugar
- 3 cups diced watermelon
- 1 cup diced cucumber
- ¼ cup diced red onion
- ½ teaspoon salt
- ½ teaspoon black pepper
- ¼ cup chopped fresh cilantro
- ½ cup crumbled feta cheese

In a small saucepan, whisk together balsamic vinegar and sugar. Cook over medium heat until reduced by half and syrupy, about 4 minutes. Allow to cool.

Meanwhile, stir together watermelon, cucumber, red onion, salt, black pepper, and cilantro. Add the balsamic reduction and feta cheese to the bowl and gently stir to combine. Serve with tortilla chips.

Makes about 4 cups

Peppered Herb Spread

- 1 (*8 ounce*) package softened cream cheese
- 1 (*4 ounce*) package softened goat cheese
- 3 tablespoons finely chopped fresh chives
- 3 tablespoons finely chopped fresh basil
- 3 tablespoons finely chopped fresh parsley
- ½ teaspoon cracked black pepper
- ¼ teaspoon red pepper flakes
- 1 clove minced garlic

Beat cream cheese and goat cheese with an electric mixer on medium speed until smooth. Add chives, basil, parsley, black pepper, red pepper flakes, and garlic and beat until combined. Transfer to a serving dish and refrigerate for at least 1 hour before serving to allow the flavors to develop. Serve with crackers or veggies.

Makes about 2 cups

Autumn Harvest Board

The colors of this board represent the taste; warm, savory, and comforting. The Autumn Harvest Board is a hit at Thanksgiving, or any other time of the year when you need a little something cozy on your table.

Cheeses: aged cheddar, blue cheese
Charcuterie: Maple Candied Bacon *(recipe below)*
Bread & Crackers: sweet potato chips, Homemade Cheese Crackers *(recipe on page 105)*
Accompaniments: pickled beets, pecans, pumpkin seeds, Granny Smith apples, pepitas
Condiments & Dips: maple syrup, spicy brown mustard
Garnish: sage

1. Put the beets, maple syrup, and spicy brown mustard in small bowls and place them on the board. Fill a bowl with sweet potato chips and place it alongside the board.
2. Arrange the aged cheddar, blue cheese, and Maple Candied Bacon on the board.
3. Nestle in a pile of Homemade Cheese Crackers.
4. Fill in any remaining gaps with pecans, pumpkin seeds, Granny Smith apple slices, and pepitas.
5. Garnish with fresh sage and serve

Maple Candied Bacon

- 2 tablespoons brown sugar
- ¼ cup maple syrup
- 1 tablespoon apple cider vinegar
- 1 pound bacon

Preheat the oven to 350°. In a small bowl, combine brown sugar, maple syrup, and apple cider vinegar. Set aside. Spread bacon on a large, rimmed baking sheet. Bake for 12 minutes, turning halfway through. Remove the bacon from the oven and brush both sides generously with the brown sugar mixture. Return to the oven and bake 5 minutes more. Brush with the sugar mixture every 5 minutes until the bacon is caramelized and crisp, about 20 minutes. Remove from the oven and set on a rack to cool.
Serves 8

Tip:
Sprinkle the apples with lemon juice to keep them from turning brown after they've been cut.

Maple Candied Bacon

Homemade Cheese Crackers, page 105

Spicy Cranberry Spread

- 1 (*12 ounce*) package cranberries
- 1 cup sugar
- 6 green onions, chopped
- ⅓ cup chopped fresh cilantro
- 1 jalapeño, seeded and finely chopped
- 1 (*8 ounce*) package cream cheese, softened

Dump cranberries and sugar into a food processor and process briefly until coarsely chopped. Transfer the mixture to a bowl and stir in green onions, cilantro, and jalapeño. Cover and refrigerate overnight.

After chilling, drain the cranberry mixture. Spread cream cheese on a plate and spoon the drained mixture over the top. Serve with crackers.

Serves 6

Homemade Cheese Crackers

- 2 tablespoons softened butter
- ¾ cup shredded sharp cheddar cheese
- ½ cup shredded Parmesan cheese
- ¼ teaspoon paprika
- ¼ teaspoon garlic salt
- ½ cup flour
- 3 tablespoons water

1. Preheat the oven to 375° and line a baking sheet with parchment paper.
2. In a mixing bowl, combine the butter, sharp cheddar cheese, Parmesan cheese, paprika, and garlic salt. Add the flour and water; stir until a dough forms.
3. Transfer the dough to a floured work surface and roll until it is about ⅛" thick. Use a pizza cutter to cut the dough into roughly 1" x 1" squares. Use a fork to poke a few holes into each cracker.
4. Arrange the crackers on the baking sheet and bake for 15 minutes or until golden brown. Let cool before transferring to an airtight container.

Makes 40

Stuffed 'Shroom Dip

- 1 tablespoon olive oil
- ½ pound ground Italian sausage
- 2 garlic cloves, minced
- 1½ pounds white button mushrooms, roughly chopped (*about 5 cups*)
- Salt & freshly ground black pepper to taste
- 1 (*8 ounce*) package cream cheese, cut into cubes
- ½ cup grated Parmesan cheese
- ⅓ cup half & half
- ½ cup chopped green onions
- 2 tablespoons unsalted butter, melted
- ¼ cup panko breadcrumbs
- ¼ cup fresh parsley, chopped

Preheat the broiler.

Heat the oil in a large skillet over medium-high heat. Add the sausage and cook, breaking into bite-sized pieces, until browned and almost cooked through. Add the garlic and cook, stirring constantly, until softened. Add in the mushrooms, salt, and a few grinds of black pepper and cook, stirring occasionally, until the mushrooms are soft, and the moisture has evaporated.

Add the cream cheese and stir until melted. Add the Parmesan, half & half, and green onions and cook, stirring occasionally, until bubbly. Pour the mushroom mixture into an oven-safe dish. Mix the butter with the panko and parsley and sprinkle on top of the mushroom mixture. Broil until the breadcrumbs are golden brown and the dip is bubbly around the edges, 5 to 10 minutes. Let sit for 10 minutes, then serve with crackers or bread.

Serves 8

Cranberry-Pistachio Cheese Ball

- 1 (*8 ounce*) package cream cheese, softened
- 2 cups shredded Monterey Jack cheese
- 1 teaspoon Dijon mustard
- 1 teaspoon Worcestershire sauce
- 1 tablespoon dried parsley
- ½ teaspoon salt
- ½ teaspoon black pepper
- ½ cup dried cranberries, roughly chopped
- ½ cup roughly chopped pistachios

Beat the cream cheese, Monterey Jack, Dijon, Worcestershire, parsley, salt, and black pepper with an electric mixer until combined. Mix in the cranberries. Cover and refrigerate until slightly firm, 1 to 2 hours.

Transfer the cheese mixture to a piece of plastic wrap. Use the plastic to shape the cheese mixture into a ball. Remove the plastic and cover the cheeseball with pistachios, pressing to adhere. Wrap in plastic wrap and chill until ready to serve. Serve with crackers.

Serves 8

Pineapple Cheese Ball

- 2 (*8 ounce*) packages softened cream cheese
- 1 (*8 ounces*) can crushed pineapple (*drained*)
- 1½ tablespoons seasoned salt
- 2 cups chopped pecans, divided
- ½ cup chopped bell pepper
- 1 tablespoon dried parsley

In a large mixing bowl, combine cream cheese, crushed pineapple, salt, 1 cup chopped pecans, bell pepper, and parsley. Chill the mixture until firm, 1 to 2 hours. Form the chilled mixture into 2 cheeseballs and roll in 1 cup chopped pecans, pressing to adhere. Wrap in plastic wrap until ready to serve. Serve with crackers.

Makes 2 cheeseballs

Holiday Bliss Board

Nothing says "holiday season" like family gatherings, and nothing is better at family gatherings than a beautiful, festive board! Pomegranates, oranges, and the delectable Cran-Orange Sauce provide the warmth, and the crackers, meats, and cheeses provide the togetherness!

Cheeses: feta, Gruyère, cranberry-cinnamon cheddar
Charcuterie: peppered salami, mesquite-smoked turkey
Bread & Crackers: Rosemary Sea Salt Crackers (*recipe on page 110*)
Accompaniments: Marcona almonds, mandarin oranges, hazelnuts, pomegranate seeds, green grapes, dried cranberries
Condiments & Dips: Cran-Orange Sauce (*recipe below*)
Garnish: rosemary

1. Put the Cran-Orange Sauce in a small bowl and place it on the board.
2. Arrange the feta, Gruyère, cranberry-cinnamon cheddar, peppered salami, and mesquite-smoked turkey on the board.
3. Nestle in a stack or two of Rosemary Sea Salt Crackers.
4. Fill in any remaining gaps with Marcona almonds, mandarin oranges, hazelnuts, pomegranate seeds, green grapes, and dried cranberries.
5. Garnish with fresh rosemary and serve.

Cran-Orange Sauce

- 1 cup orange juice
- ½ cup sugar
- ¼ teaspoon salt
- 1 (*12 ounce*) bag of fresh cranberries
- Zest of ½ orange, plus more for garnish

Bring orange juice, sugar, and salt to a boil in a medium saucepan. Add fresh cranberries and the zest of ½ orange; return to a boil. Reduce heat to low and simmer, uncovered, until the cranberries split, and the sauce thickens. Cool to room temperature and serve. Garnish with orange zest.

Makes 2 cups

Tip:
Rosemary is the perfect winter-themed garnish because it resembles pine greenery.

Cran-Orange Sauce

Rosemary Sea Salt
Crackers, page 110

Rosemary Sea Salt Crackers

- 1½ cups flour, plus more for dusting
- 1 teaspoon sea salt, plus more for sprinkling
- 1 teaspoon sugar
- 1 tablespoon dried rosemary
- 3 tablespoons olive oil, plus more for brushing
- ½ cup water

1. Preheat oven to 475° and line a baking sheet with parchment paper.
2. Whisk together the flour, sea salt, sugar, and dried rosemary. Add olive oil and water; stir until fully combined.
3. Turn the dough out onto a lightly floured surface. Roll out until it is about ⅛" thick, adding flour as needed to keep the dough from sticking to the rolling pin. Trim the thin edges of the dough to keep them from burning. Cut into roughly 2"x 1" rectangles with a pizza cutter. Brush with olive oil and sprinkle with a pinch of sea salt.
4. Arrange crackers in a single layer on the baking sheet. Bake for 13 to 17 minutes or until golden brown. Store in an airtight container at room temperature for up to 1 week.

Makes 40

Cream Cheese & Lox

- 1 (*8 ounce*) package cream cheese, softened
- ½ cup sour cream
- ½ teaspoon garlic powder
- 1 teaspoon dried minced onion
- ½ teaspoon poppy seeds
- ½ teaspoon sesame seeds, plus more for garnish
- ¼ red onion, finely chopped
- 3 ounces lox, chopped
- 1 tablespoon capers, roughly chopped (*optional*)
- 1 teaspoon chopped fresh dill, plus more for garnish

Stir together the cream cheese, sour cream, garlic powder, minced onion, poppy seeds, sesame seeds, red onion, lox, capers, and fresh dill. Refrigerate for 30 minutes to allow flavors to develop. Garnish with fresh dill and sesame seeds. Serve with bagels or bagel chips.

Makes about 2 cups

Bagel Brunch Board

The Bagel Brunch Board is a fun way to deconstruct breakfast. Provide several different types of bagels to satisfy every craving!

Cheeses: cream cheese, Garlic & Herb Boursin, Brie
Charcuterie: Nova lox, prosciutto
Bread & Crackers: Any bagel you want (*we used plain and everything bagels*)
Accompaniments: Pickled Red Onions (*recipe below*), green onions, capers, avocados, cucumbers, raspberries, blueberries, arugula
Condiments & Dips: raspberry jam
Garnish: dill

1 Put the cream cheese, Pickled Red Onions, green onions, capers, and raspberry jam in bowls and place them on the board.

2 Arrange the Boursin, Brie, lox, and prosciutto on the board.

3 Cut the bagels into quarters and stack them on the board.

4 Fill in any remaining gaps with sliced avocado, sliced cucumber, raspberries, blueberries, and arugula.

5 Garnish with fresh dill and serve

Pickled Red Onions

- 1 red onion, thinly sliced
- ½ cup apple cider vinegar
- 1 tablespoon sugar
- 1½ teaspoons salt
- 1 cup hot water

Place the onion slices inside a jar. In a measuring cup, combine apple cider vinegar, sugar, salt, and hot water. Pour the pickling mixture over the sliced onions and let them sit for an hour at room temperature. Cover and chill in the refrigerator for at least 2 hours before serving. Store in the refrigerator for up to 3 weeks.

Makes about 1 pint

Tip:
Pickled red onions are versatile in the kitchen—use them to add a burst of flavor to tacos, hamburgers, hot dogs, and more.

Pickled Red Onions

Bagels & Lox Butter Board

When guests see the Bagels & Lox Butter Board on the table, there's only a matter of time before every bit of butter is gone. Packed with savory flavors and served with toasty bagels, this butter board is a crowd-pleaser.

- 2 cups of unsalted butter, softened at room temperature
- ⅛ cup fresh dill weed, chopped, and ⅛ cup for garnish, leave in sprigs
- 1 tablespoon everything bagel seasoning
- 1 (*3-ounce*) jar capers, drained well
- 1 shallot or ½ red onion, sliced very thinly
- 1 pint cherry or grape tomatoes, halved or quartered, depending on size
- 1 (*4 ounces*) pack smoked salmon, sliced thinly
- Flaky sea salt or kosher salt
- 6–10 bagels
- 2 bags bagel chips

1. Let butter sit out at room temperature overnight. Do not microwave. Butter should be softened, not melted. Add butter to a medium size mixing bowl.
2. Chop fresh dill weed finely. Add to butter and mix thoroughly.
3. Add everything bagel seasoning and mix. (*If not using the butter immediately, cover and chill in the fridge until ready to use, up to 12 hours. Let butter sit out at room temperature for several hours prior to use.*)
4. Spread butter onto wooden board leaving a 2- to 3-inch border on each side. (*You may spread butter onto cut-to-size parchment paper on the board for easier clean-up.*)
5. Top butter with thin layer of salt, well-drained capers, shallot/onion, tomatoes, salmon, and dill sprigs.
6. Arrange bagel chips and bagels along the borders of the board for dipping.

Serves 6 – 8

Breakfast of Champions Board

Breakfast is the most important meal of the day—especially when it's the Breakfast of Champions Board! This board has a little bit of everything; sweet, savory, fresh, and crunchy, your guests will be asking for this board for every meal.

Cheeses: garden vegetable cream cheese, Gouda, extra sharp white cheddar
Charcuterie: bacon, sausage patties
Bread & Crackers: bagel chips, pumpernickel bread, rye bread
Accompaniments: Honeycrisp apples, hard-boiled eggs, strawberries, sweet mini bells, blueberries
Condiments & Dips: Garlic-Chive Butter (*recipe below*), apple butter
Garnish: dill, chives

1 Put the garden vegetable cream cheese, Garlic-Chive Butter, and apple butter in small bowls and place them on the board.

2 Arrange the Gouda, extra sharp white cheddar, bacon, and sausage on the board.

3 Nestle in some bagel chips, sliced pumpernickel, and sliced rye.

4 Fill in any remaining gaps with Honeycrisp apples, hard-boiled eggs, strawberries, sweet mini bells, and blueberries.

5 Garnish with fresh dill and chives.

Garlic-Chive Butter

- ½ cup softened butter
- 1 teaspoon minced garlic
- 1 tablespoon chopped fresh chives
- ½ teaspoon dried parsley
- ¼ teaspoon black pepper

Combine ingredients in a bowl. Whisk until fully combined. Let rest for at least 1 hour to allow the flavors to meld.
Makes ½ cup

Tip:
For a sweet butter, swap out the garlic, chives, parsley, and black pepper for ½ teaspoon cinnamon, ¼ teaspoon vanilla, and 1 tablespoon honey.

Garlic-Chive Butter

Fruit Salsa

- 2 tablespoons sugar
- 1 tablespoon brown sugar
- 3 tablespoons fruit preserves, any flavor (*we used raspberry*)
- 2 kiwis, peeled & diced
- 2 Golden Delicious apples, diced
- 1 (*6 ounce*) package fresh raspberries
- 1 pound of fresh strawberries, diced
- 1 cup fresh blueberries

In a big bowl, mix the sugar, brown sugar, and preserves until well combined. Add the kiwis, apples, raspberries, strawberries, and blueberries; gently stir to mix. Cover and chill until ready to serve. Serve with **Cinnamon Chips.**
Serves a crowd

Cinnamon Chips

- 10 tortillas
- ⅛ cup sugar
- ½ teaspoon cinnamon

Preheat the oven to 350°. Coat 10 (*10-inch*) tortillas with cooking spray. Sprinkle with cinnamon-sugar and spritz again with cooking spray. Cut each tortilla into eight wedges and arrange in a single layer on baking sheets. Bake on the bottom oven rack for 10 to 15 minutes, until lightly browned; cool before serving.
Makes 80 chips.

Sweet

The boards in this section focus more on flavors that are sweet and indulgent. These boards are wonderfully paired with a savory board–or even another sweet board! It's also always a good idea to offset the flavors of your board with opposite-flavored dips and accompaniments. Feel free to mix and match the recipes in this section with those in the savory section to satisfy all cravings!

Sweet Brie Board

The Sweet Brie Board is warm and soft in the best way. Gooey Honey-Almond Brie, salty prosciutto, and a crisp, sweet apple makes the perfect bite on a scrumptious board.

Cheeses: Honey-Almond Brie (*recipe below*)
Charcuterie: prosciutto, Genoa salami
Bread & Crackers: Toasted Baguette Slices (*recipe on page 50*)
Accompaniments: golden raisins, pistachios, red grapes, Honeycrisp apples
Condiments & Dips: peach preserves
Garnish: rosemary

1 Put the golden raisins, pistachios, and peach preserves in bowls and place them around the board.
2 Arrange the prosciutto and Genoa salami on the board.
3 Add a few stacks of toasted baguette slices.
4 Fill in any remaining gaps with red grapes and sliced Honeycrisp apples.
5 Garnish with fresh rosemary.
6 Place the baked Brie beside the board and serve.

Honey-Almond Brie

- 1 (*8-ounce*) wheel of Brie
- ¼ cup honey
- 2 sprigs rosemary
- ½ cup chopped roasted almonds

Preheat oven to 350°. Use a knife to trim the thin white rind off the top of the wheel of Brie. Place the Brie in an oven-safe ramekin or skillet. Bake for 11 to 13 minutes or until softened. While the Brie bakes, combine honey and a sprig of rosemary in a small saucepan over low heat. Once warmed, stir in almonds. Spoon the honey mixture over the Brie and garnish with remaining sprig of rosemary.
Serves 6

Tip:
The cheese loses its "gooeyness" relatively fast, so try to time it to come out of the oven right as guests arrive.

Honey-Almond Brie

Cinnamon Honey Butter Board

Soft, cinnamon butter drizzled with honey is the perfect companion
to the Sweet Brie Board. Dip in cinnamon raisin bread or gingersnap
cookies, and you might be surprised at how fast it goes!

- 2 cups unsalted butter, softened at room temperature
- 3 tablespoons honey for butter, 2 tablespoons honey for drizzling
- ½ teaspoon ground cinnamon
- 1 teaspoon powdered sugar
- ¼ teaspoon vanilla extract
- 2 ounces pecans, chopped into large pieces
- Loaf of cinnamon raisin bread, cut into bite-sized pieces
- Shortbread cookies
- Ginger snap cookies

1. Let butter sit out at room temperature overnight. Do not microwave. Butter should be softened, not melted. Add butter to a medium size mixing bowl and whip until light and fluffy.
2. Add 2 tablespoons honey (*saving 1 tablespoon for later*), powdered sugar, ground cinnamon, and vanilla extract. Mix thoroughly. (*If not using the butter immediately, cover and chill in the fridge until ready to use, up to 12 hours. Let butter sit out at room temperature for several hours prior to use.*)
3. Spread butter onto a wooden board leaving a 2- to 3-inch border on each side. (*You may spread butter onto cut-to-size parchment paper on the board for easier clean-up.*)
4. Top butter with thin layer of chopped pecans.
5. Drizzle reserved honey on top of butter and pecans.
6. Arrange bread and cookies along the borders of the board for dipping.

Serves 6–8

Berries Galore Board

The sweet Whipped Honey Ricotta combined with the tart berries on this board are the perfect pairing. A slice of cheese along with it? Berry good indeed.

Cheeses: Whipped Honey Ricotta *(recipe below)*, sharp white cheddar, blueberry cheddar
Bread & Crackers: cinnamon-raisin bread
Accompaniments: blueberries, blackberries, raspberries, strawberries, walnuts, golden raisins
Condiments & Dips: cherry preserves
Garnish: mint

1 Put the Whipped Honey Ricotta, blueberries, blackberries, and cherry preserves in small bowls and place them on the board.

2 Arrange the sharp white cheddar and blueberry cheddar on the board.

3 Cut each slice of cinnamon raisin bread into quarters and place on the board.

4 Fill in any remaining gaps on the board with raspberries, strawberries, walnuts, and golden raisins.

5 Garnish with fresh mint and serve.

Whipped Honey Ricotta

- 2 cups ricotta cheese
- 1 (*4 ounce*) package cream cheese, softened
- 1 tablespoon sugar
- ¼ cup honey, plus more for garnish
- ¼ teaspoon vanilla extract
- Juice of ½ lemon

Blend ingredients in a food processor until smooth. Transfer to a bowl and refrigerate until ready to serve. Drizzle with extra honey before serving.
Makes 2½ cups

Whipped Honey Ricotta

Yogurt Parfait Board

The hands-on Yogurt Parfait Board becomes more fun if you set out
bowls and spoons and let guests build their own customized parfaits!

Base: vanilla yogurt, strawberry yogurt
Accompaniments: Maple Granola (*recipe
below*), strawberries, blueberries, raspberries,
kiwis, bananas, pecans, pepitas, chocolate-
covered raisins
Garnish: mint

1 Put the yogurt and the Maple Granola in
bowls and place them on the board.

2 Fill in any remaining gaps with
strawberries, blueberries, raspberries,
kiwis, bananas, pecans, pepitas, and
chocolate-covered raisins.

3 Garnish with fresh mint and serve.

Maple Granola

- 2 cups old-fashioned oats
- ½ cup chopped pecans
- ¼ cup sunflower seeds
- ¼ cup maple syrup
- 3 tablespoons olive oil
- ½ teaspoon vanilla extract
- ¼ teaspoon salt

Preheat the oven to 300°. In a large mixing bowl, combine
ingredients. Spread the mixture in a thin layer on a
baking sheet lined with parchment paper. Bake for
25 minutes. Cool before storing or serving. Store in an
airtight container for up to 2 weeks.
Makes 2½ cups

Maple Granola

Tip:
This recipe makes a lot of dip. Consider dividing into smaller portions and freezing some for later. Then just thaw and dip.

Zesty Lime Dip

- 1 (*8 ounce*) package cream cheese, softened
- 1 (*14 ounce*) can sweetened condensed milk
- 1 (*6 ounce*) container key lime yogurt
- 1 (*6 ounce*) container piña colada yogurt
- 1 teaspoon vanilla
- 1 tablespoon lemon juice
- 1 lime

Beat cream cheese in a big mixing bowl on medium speed until very creamy. Beat in sweetened condensed milk, key lime yogurt, piña colada yogurt, vanilla, and lemon juice until light and smooth; stir in the zest and juice of the lime. Cover and refrigerate overnight. Serve with fruit (*we used strawberries, orange segments, and pineapple chunks*).

Makes 4 cups

Caramel Apple Dip

- ½ cup chopped pecans
- 1 (*8 ounce*) cream cheese, softened
- 4 apples
- Lemon juice
- ½ cup caramel sauce

Tip:
If you're in a hurry, just pour on the caramel sauce without heating and toss on the pecans without toasting. It'll still be delicious!

Put chopped pecans in a dry skillet and toast over medium heat for 8 minutes, stirring occasionally.

Set cream cheese on a serving tray. Core and slice apples (*mix & match your favorites*) and put into a bowl; drizzle with lemon juice, stir to coat, and then drain. Heat caramel sauce in the microwave and drizzle it over the cream cheese. Top with the toasted pecans and surround with the sliced apples.

Serves 8

PB & Chocolate Hummus

- 1 (*16 ounce*) can chickpeas (*drained & rinsed*)
- ¼ cup peanut butter
- ¼ cup honey, plus more for garnish
- 2 tablespoons maple syrup
- ½ cup unsweetened cocoa powder
- 1 teaspoon vanilla
- ¼ teaspoon salt
- 2–3 tablespoons water

In a food processor, combine chickpeas, peanut butter, honey, maple syrup, cocoa powder, vanilla, and salt. Process for 30 seconds, then scrape down the sides of the bowl. Add water and process again until it becomes nice and creamy; chill.

Set out to soften 30 minutes before serving. Drizzle with honey and top with chopped peanuts. Serve with pretzels and fresh fruit.

Serves 6

Fruit Lovers Board

The Fruit Lovers Board perfectly balances sweet, juicy fruits with acidic, tart ones. Lovers of both will find something to delight in, whether it be the fruit by itself or paired with cheese, chocolate, or Delectable Fruit Dip!

Cheeses: Brie, sharp cheddar, white cheddar
Bread & Crackers: toasted cinnamon-raisin bread, woven wheat crackers
Accompaniments: Honeycrisp apples, pears, kiwis, strawberries, mandarin oranges, almonds, dark chocolate, vanilla wafers, red grapes
Condiments & Dips: Delectable Fruit Dip (*recipe below*), honey

1 Put the Delectable Fruit Dip and honey in bowls and place them on the board.

2 Arrange the Brie, sharp cheddar, and white cheddar on the board.

3 Add some toasted cinnamon-raisin bread and woven wheat crackers.

4 Fill in any remaining gaps with sliced Honeycrisp apple, sliced pear, sliced kiwi, strawberries, sliced mandarin oranges, almonds, dark chocolate, vanilla wafers, and red grapes.

Delectable Fruit Dip

- 1 (*8 ounce*) package cream cheese, softened
- 1 cup plain yogurt
- ½ cup brown sugar
- ¼ teaspoon cinnamon
- 1 teaspoon vanilla extract

Add cream cheese to a mixing bowl and beat on low speed until smooth. Slowly add yogurt and continue to mix until combined. Add brown sugar, cinnamon, and vanilla extract; mix until combined. Cover and place in the refrigerator for at least 1 hour before serving.
Makes 1½ cups

Tip:
Gouda, goat cheese, and fresh mozzarella also pair well with fruit.

Delectable Fruit Dip

Chocolate Galore Board

Nothing says "sweet" like the Chocolate Galore Board. Rich dark chocolate paired with Brie and Hazelnut Mascarpone Spread will please the chocolate lover, while the pairing of fresh fruit, salty nuts, and gooey honey will entice even those who aren't the biggest chocolate fans.

Cheese: Brie
Bread & Crackers: sliced baguette
Accompaniments: chocolate-covered raisins, raspberries, blueberries, green grapes, almonds, roasted peanuts, dark chocolate
Condiments & Dips: Hazelnut-Mascarpone Spread (*recipe below*), honey
Garnish: mint

1 Put the Hazelnut-Mascarpone Spread and honey in bowls and place them around the board
2 Place the Brie on the board.
3 Add a few slices of baguette.
4 Fill in any remaining gaps with chocolate-covered raisins, raspberries, blueberries, green grapes, almonds, roasted peanuts, and dark chocolate.
5 Garnish with fresh mint and serve.

Hazelnut-Mascarpone Spread

- 1 cup chocolate-hazelnut spread
- 1 cup mascarpone
- 1 (*4 ounce*) package cream cheese, softened
- Sea salt to taste
- Chopped hazelnuts

In a large mixing bowl, combine ingredients with an electric mixer. Transfer to a serving dish and top with chopped hazelnuts and sea salt.
Makes 2½ cups

Tip:
Cheddar and Monterey Jack also pair surprisingly well with chocolate.

Hazelnut-Mascarpone Spread

Cookie Dough Dip

- 1 (*8 ounce*) package cream cheese, softened
- ½ cup unsalted butter, softened
- 1 teaspoon vanilla extract
- 1 cup creamy peanut butter
- 3 tablespoons brown sugar
- 1 cup powdered sugar
- ½ cup oatmeal
- ½ cup miniature M&Ms
- 1 cup miniature semisweet chocolate chips

With an electric mixer, beat the cream cheese, butter, vanilla, and peanut butter until smooth. Mix in the brown sugar and powdered sugar until combined. Next fold in oatmeal, M&Ms, and chocolate chips. Serve with graham crackers, fruit, or pretzels.

Makes about 3 cups

Tiramisu Dip

- 1 (*8 ounce*) package softened cream cheese
- ¾ cup mascarpone cheese
- ½ cup powdered sugar
- 1 teaspoon vanilla extract
- 2 teaspoons instant coffee
- Cocoa powder

Beat cream cheese and mascarpone with an electric mixer on medium speed until smooth. Add powdered sugar and mix for 1 minute. Add vanilla extract and instant coffee and mix until fully incorporated. Scoop the dip into a serving dish and sprinkle with cocoa powder. Serve with vanilla wafers, fruit, or pretzels.

Makes 2 cups

Index